"*Meeting God in the Bible* n
the world of devotional lite
is unique in its combination ∪ı contemporary (ACTS) and ancient (*Lectio Divina*) practices with sound hermeneutical principles and presentation in a narrative style reminiscent of C.S. Lewis's *Letters to Malcolm, Chiefly on Prayer*. The book reads less like an information manual and more like a rich and lively conversation with a wise spiritual mentor. It is a great resource for churches looking to train their congregants in a rich and life-giving devotional life, as well as a wonderful book to give new and old believers alike."

Joshua **Swanson** (DMin), Lead Pastor of Christ Church Sierra Madre, CA

"John has written a very practical guide for one-on-one discipleship using the Word of God. He identifies and demonstrates many practices that help one meet God in the Scriptures and illustrates how they might be applied by tracing these practices in the lives of two fictional characters. Their discussions open the door to many questions people encounter when using the Bible and offers practical answers. This is a very helpful tool for Quiet Times and Bible-based discipleship."

The Rt. Rev. Dr. Mark Zimmerman, Bishop of the Anglican Diocese of the Southwest

"*Meeting God in the Bible* is a fun, engaging, and practical guide for how to grow in your relationship with Jesus. Along the way, John also gives great vision for how to lead others into a growing relationship with Jesus. This book is a wonderful discipleship tool for new and seasoned believers alike."

Chad Francis, Lead Pastor of Hope Church, Albuquerque, NM

"John Linebarger's book starts by understanding that people are humans before they are Christians. It leads gently into a path of prayerfully reading Scripture as a meaningful and motivating encounter with the living God while being in the midst of our busy and distracting lives.

It is especially relevant for new believers. It can be difficult for those who have not grown up in the culture of evangelical Christianity to navigate a new life tuned to Jesus, and to decipher Biblical language in a way that is useful for doing God's will in daily life. Through the narrative of Victoria and Sharon, the reader is introduced to the traditional Christian ways of learning from the Bible how to walk the discipline of the Christian life. John also notes that proper evangelism is not a strategy but a story, and the hero of the story is Jesus Christ, not me. The book includes a study guide, which is helpful in particular for group use and for working through the steps leading to a prayerful and Biblical Christian lifestyle."

The Rt. Rev. Win Mott, retired bishop in the Anglican Church in North America and the author of *The Earth is the Lord's: Nothing is Secular*

"John Linebarger has written an engaging and informative work on the devotional use of the Bible within an evangelical context. It is engaging and slips past one's defenses because it is embedded in a realistic narrative of a pastor's wife who is mentoring a new convert. It is evangelical Protestant insofar as that is the religious language used, that is the choice of biblical translations, that is the choice of reading methods and hermeneutical tools, and that is the group for whom the Scriptures are the means God uses to speak to us. It is also up-to-date in that it uses journaling and *Lectio Divina*, as understood within that world. This is a book that one could hand to a new convert. This is a book that one might read oneself for a 'refresher' on the basics. It is realistic, warm, and approachable. I recommend it for those evangelical Protestants wishing to grow in their spiritual life."

Rev. Peter H. Davids (PhD), New Testament Editor, Word Biblical Commentary

Meeting God in the Bible

How to Read Scripture Devotionally

Meeting God in the Bible

How to Read Scripture Devotionally

JOHN M. LINEBARGER

Fontes Press

Meeting God in the Bible:
How to Read Scripture Devotionally

Copyright © 2019 by John M. Linebarger

ISBN-13: 978-1-948048-12-5

FONTES PRESS

DALLAS, TX

www.fontespress.com

To the congregation at Church of Our Lord,
who prayed for me.
To my Life Group at Hope Church,
who challenged me.
And to my family,
who loved me and supported me.

CONTENTS

FOREWORD

FERNANDO ORTEGA

As I sit down to write this foreword, the world is halfway through the year 2019. Like any given date in history, there are global crises everywhere to read about in the newspapers or online: global warming; a heart-breaking civil war in Yemen; a brutal dictatorship in Venezuela; family separations at the U.S./Mexico border. All these crises and many more come to mind.

Four decades ago, when I was in my twenties, I often tried to imagine what life would be like at the turn of the twentieth century. I would be 43! What would it be like to be so old? Would I be a father? Would I own a house? Would my faith be intact? The answer to all the questions would be "yes," though the last question is somewhat abstract, both in how it is asked and in how I would answer it.

When I was in my twenties, "Quiet Times" were part of my daily routine. I studied the Bible, memorized scripture passages, read devotional books, kept in fellowship with my fellow Christians, and attended worship services. I always look back on my days at Hoffmantown Baptist Church with fondness and great nostalgia. They were the most healthy and functional days of my

Christian journey thus far. They were also the beginning of my
career as a professional church musician, recording artist, song-
writer, and arranger. Alas—when the church is part of one's pro-
fession, complications are sure to follow, as I was soon to find out.

Over the years I have walked with various congregations
through every type of church scandal, including extramarital af-
fairs, embezzlement of church funds, addictions, divorces, in-
fighting—not to mention some of the personal catastrophes that
plagued me. These events have, on occasion, pummeled me,
blindsided me, undone me, and left me curled up on the floor and
hyperventilating as I waited for a word from God. Now, at 62
years of age, it's impossible not to feel jaded—sometimes
deeply—as I try to navigate the road ahead in my walk with the
Lord Jesus. Evangelical Christianity as I knew it in my twenties is
in crisis, not just for the reasons I stated above, but also because
the world has in many ways jettisoned religion and spirituality as
an answer to its questions.

The last time I visited England, Scotland, and Ireland, I was
astonished at how many beautiful, centuries-old churches and
cathedrals were now abandoned or had been converted into res-
taurants, bars, nightclubs, or dance halls. That scenario has
played out over most of Europe. To a lesser degree, the same is
happening here in the United States. Granted, the Church is
more than just a building, but this phenomenon is definitely a
symptom of an overall turn away from Christianity all over the
traditionally Christian world.

I found it interesting that this European turn from Christianity, the world's global crises, and my own spiritual journey right
through the middle of it all came to mind when I first started to
read John Linebarger's book. During my reading I felt aware of
the soft erosions in my own faith over the years—the many
places where I've let my guard down and given myself over to

doubts, fears, anxieties and sadness. I found myself resisting the enthusiasm of the characters in this book, resisting the joy that John Linebarger seemed to have in telling the story. But there were certain sentences and phrases that made me stop and read them over again. For instance, when I came to Sharon studying a passage in Philippians and . . . "She read this passage over and over, bathing in it, reveling in it, drinking it in like water to a thirsty soul," I remember thinking, "That used to be me! What ever happened to that eager, thirsty Bible reading?"

At the end of the same section of the book, the Philippians passage is described as "God's recipe for mental health." I thought immediately of my several-years-long struggle with anxiety and social phobias. There were days on end where it seemed like I was walking on my hands and knees asking God for relief from the anxious thoughts that plagued and crippled me. I would go to the sanctuary of the church where I worked, kneel in the pews asking God to get me through just 10 more minutes, just 5 more minutes, and then head back into the office for a little while before returning to the sanctuary to kneel in the pews again. That's the way I crawled my way through life and through my walk with God.

As I look back on those exceedingly difficult and agonizing days, I'm grateful for my pastor Josh Swanson who gently and persistently nudged me towards God. He was much like Sharon, the pastor's wife in this book. He prayed with me, gave me books to read and Bible passages to mull over, which were small steps that helped me to not lose hope. I thought about him several times as I read this very helpful and, for me, very timely book.

What does *Meeting God in the Bible* have to do with abandoned cathedrals, church scandals, and an anxiety-plagued musician? First off, I wish I had read this book when I was eighteen or so. I wish I'd had a very practical guide back then that taught me how to orchestrate my times alone with God. I was very good in those days about spending large amounts of time reading the Scriptures, but I easily glazed over the passages, not looking to experience God in them. My daily routine in reading and prayer did not prepare me for the scandal that was about to happen in my church.

It was the mid-1970s and I played piano at a Pentecostal church that was vibrant and alive. Our congregation was mostly young. We were ardent, faithful, and zealous followers of Jesus. We hung on every word that our leaders spoke. It was a devastating blow to us when our pastor ran off with a teenage girl who was just a couple of years older than me. Soon after, his wife took over the church and it was not long before she had become addicted to prescription drugs and was embezzling church funds. Our tears flowed on the altar as we knelt before God, trying to figure out how the leaders we had trusted and believed in could so easily fall into sinfulness. The church services in the aftermath became more and more bizarre. My closest friends started to leave the church and abandon Christianity altogether.

My parents lived in Honduras at that time and I flew down to visit them for a few weeks. One night I was walking on the beach and felt completely overwhelmed by the church situation back home. I knelt in the sand as the waves washed me over and declared to God that I could no longer believe in him. I sobbed and cried out, "If this is Christianity, I don't want it! If this is what it means to follow, then I just can't do it!"

For several months I lived as though God did not exist. It wasn't the last time I would place my faith in people over God. I wonder now how differently I might have handled the situation had I learned to meet God in his Word. To connect with Him who is greater than me, greater than every hardship, and infinitely more powerful than the dark forces that were at work in the leadership of my church. What would it have been like to find Him in his Word, to hear Him speak to me, comfort me, and encourage me, instead of me falling into despair?

I don't recall what kind of books were available to me in those early days of my faith. There was Hannah Hurnard's book called *Hind's Feet on High Places*. It was a good and helpful read, though fairly abstract in its approach. I think I found it a bit precious and sentimental, in retrospect. I had not yet discovered C.S. Lewis—he wasn't really a staple in the Charismatic Movement. I imagine we would have thought of him as too cerebral and, audaciously, considered him to not be "filled with the Spirit." Whatever the case, I had no guide like the one John Linebarger has written here.

I humbly, but confidently recommend this book to anyone. It is well written, insightful, and though short, fairly comprehensive. There is something here for every Christian, no matter how new or old to the faith.

How to Use This Book

This book consists of several components intended to reinforce the learning process of reading Scripture devotionally.

- ➤ An extended story that constitutes most of the book.
- ➤ An annotated bibliography for further reading.
- ➤ A study guide for each of the chapters of the book. The study guide was created with Sunday school classes, small groups, and home groups in mind, but it can be equally useful for individual study.
- ➤ A helpful summary of all of the major topics in the book in Appendix 1.
- ➤ A short biblical theology of story in Appendix 2. This appendix is intended both to motivate the choice of story as the literary vehicle for the book itself as well as to encourage you to share your own story in proclaiming the gospel. Story is a powerful and pervasive communication mechanism in Scripture.

Visit fontespress.com/meetinggod for helpful resources and links related to the major topics of the book. The website will be updated periodically as new resources become available.

ENCOUNTERING GOD
IN A QUIET TIME

"So what do I do now?" Victoria said, her voice rising in urgency. She was sitting in a coffee shop with Sharon, the wife of the pastor of her church, talking about her recent decision to trust Jesus Christ as her Savior and Lord.

"Well," replied Sharon, "what you've just done is to begin a relationship with Jesus. And like any relationship, you need to spend time with Jesus in order for the relationship to grow."

"How do I do that?" asked Victoria. "I mean, Jennifer told me that I needed to read the Bible and pray and go to church and stuff, but I'm not really sure how to do that the right way." Jennifer was a close friend of Victoria's. Over time Jennifer had shared her own faith in Jesus, which inspired Victoria to put her trust in Jesus as well. It was Jennifer who suggested that Victoria meet with Sharon to be mentored in her new-found faith.

Sharon looked thoughtful for a moment. "There are a lot of ways to go about this, but the first way I'd recommend is to make a habit of having a Quiet Time with Jesus."

"What's a Quiet Time?" Victoria thought she might have heard Jennifer use those words before, but she didn't really know what they meant.

"A Quiet Time is just a name for time that you spend alone with God. You read the Bible, because that's how God talks to you. You pray, because that's how you talk to God. And with God's help you change things in your life, both big things and little things, because of your conversations with God. In one way it's like any other important relationship in your life. You and the other person talk openly, honestly, and frequently. And those conversations change you."

Victoria looked puzzled. She stared blankly at her half-finished cup of coffee, struggling to understand what a Quiet Time meant. "I'm not quite sure how I would do that with God."

"Let me get a bit more specific," Sharon continued. "Perhaps the best time to have a Quiet Time is first thing in the morning. This will depend on you, of course, and mornings don't work for everybody. The important thing is to pick a consistent time every day. But the Bible itself seems to indicate that mornings are a good time to meet God. You can think of it as 'waking up with God.' For example, here's a verse in the Psalms that talks about meeting God in the morning." Sharon tapped on the Bible app on her phone and read a verse from Psalm 5. "'O LORD, in the morning you hear my voice; in the morning I prepare a sacrifice for you and watch.'"[1]

Since Victoria still seemed a bit confused, Sharon added, "And it was Jesus' own habit to get up in the morning and spend time with his Father. Let me find one of those passages for you." Three taps later, Sharon read a verse from the first chapter of the Gospel of Mark. "'And rising very early in the morning, while it was still dark, he departed and went out to a desolate place, and there he prayed.'"[2]

"OK, let's say I try to get up in the morning to have a Quiet Time," Victoria interjected, a bit impatiently. She wasn't really a morning person. "What do I actually *do* during a Quiet Time?"

"I was getting to that," Sharon responded gently. "Let me tell you some things that have worked for me in getting to know God by spending time with him. First, start off with prayer. Pray something like, 'Dear God, by the power of your Holy Spirit who inspired your Word, please speak to me and strengthen me to change my life because of what you have said.' Then pick a short passage of Scripture and read it slowly several times. Meditate on what you've just read by asking yourself these three questions: 'What does this passage tell me about God? What does this passage tell me about myself, or about humanity of which I am a part? And with God's help, how should my life be changed so that I can become more like God?' Finally, end your Quiet Time in prayer, the way it began, by thanking God for meeting you in his Word and asking him again for the strength to change your life to please him. This closing prayer is also a great place to make requests of God, both for you and for other people, and to thank him and praise him for who he is and what he has done."

"Hmm," mused Victoria. "About how long should a Quiet Time take?"

"Well, that depends. Initially, while you're getting used to it and trying to establish a daily habit, you might want to spend only about 15 minutes in a Quiet Time, 10 minutes reading the Bible and five minutes in prayer. When you get more experienced, your Quiet Time could become longer by spending more time in reading and prayer until it reaches 30 minutes or more. It would depend on your schedule and what you're going through at the time."

Victoria pursed her lips. "On some days that might be really hard to do. But maybe it would be easier on weekends."

"For me, it's just the reverse." Sifting through the experiences that suddenly flooded her mind, Sharon hurriedly clarified what she had said earlier. "Oh, there's a danger that you'll want to avoid. The danger is to spend most of your time just reading and studying Scripture instead of meditating on Scripture, meeting God in Scripture, and praying. If all you do is read and study, then the whole experience can become more of an academic exercise than an occasion to meet God in his Word and to live differently because of that meeting. There's certainly a place for reading Scripture academically, especially if you want to understand the content of the Bible and its original meaning. But the goal of a Quiet Time is to read the Bible *devotionally*, not just *academically*. Maybe you can use these verses from the first psalm as a model." She quickly tapped her way to the beginning of the book of Psalms and began to read.

> Blessed is the man
> who walks not in the counsel of the wicked,
> nor stands in the way of sinners,
> nor sits in the seat of scoffers;
> but his delight is in the law of the LORD,
> and on his law he meditates day and night.
> He is like a tree
> planted by streams of water
> that yields its fruit in its season,
> and its leaf does not wither.
> In all that he does, he prospers.[3]

Sharon anticipated Victoria's reaction by saying, "Of course, every time you see the word 'man' think 'man and woman,' and every time you see 'he' think 'he or she.' That's actually the intent of the psalm, to apply what it says to everybody. But look at what the psalm teaches about the Word of God, which is what the word 'law' is really referring to here: if you continually meditate on God's Word, and even delight in it, then it will make your life strong, rooted, and fruitful. Your meditation on the Word will literally change your life. And in some way, at least, you will prosper. Just don't expect money to rain down from the sky, because that's not what the psalm is promising."

Victoria laughed. "It's hard to imagine that anyone becomes a Christian for the money. And most of the pastors that I've met seem to be just scraping by."

Sharon smiled and chose not to pursue that thought. She tapped again on her phone. "Even if you read the Bible devotionally, the book of James describes a trap you can fall into if you don't ask all three questions that I recommended. What happens is that you become a hearer rather than a doer, and fail to be changed by anything that happened in your Quiet Time. Let me read you what James has to say."

> But be doers of the word, and not hearers only, deceiving yourselves. For if anyone is a hearer of the word and not a doer, he is like a man who looks intently at his natural face in a mirror. For he looks at himself and goes away and at once forgets what he was like. But the one who looks into the perfect law, the law of liberty, and perseveres, being no hearer who forgets but a doer who acts, he will be blessed in his doing.[4]

As Sharon was reading Victoria was taking notes in a small notebook. When Sharon finished, Victoria looked up and flashed a smile. "Thank you for this, Sharon. Let me try this out sometime tomorrow. Where in the Bible should I start?"

"Why don't you start with the Gospel of John? It paints a

unique picture of Jesus that I think you'd really enjoy." The two women talked some more, about their backgrounds and families and future plans. Victoria thanked Sharon again, and they both left the coffee shop.

1

READING SCRIPTURE DEVOTIONALLY

The Bible is a treasure, given by God through humans so that humans can think rightly about God. Theologians call this form of divine revelation "special revelation" to contrast it with the general revelation of the nature of God that is perceived through what he has created. Yet claiming that the Bible teaches truths about God can obscure the reality that the Bible is personal encounter as well, a place where we can meet God in his Word and experience his presence in our lives. Through the Bible God can speak with us, enlighten us, encourage us, rebuke us, and embrace us. The Bible is not just a book for the head; instead, it is also a book for the heart and the hands. The human will and behavior are impacted by the Bible, not just the mind. The words of Psalm 119 point this out particularly well.

> Oh how I love your law!
>   It is my meditation all the day.
> How sweet are your words to my taste,
>   sweeter than honey to my mouth!
> Through your precepts I get understanding;
>   therefore I hate every false way.[5]

In short, the Bible is intended to be read devotionally and practically, not just academically.

In the pages that follow, several approaches to reading the Bible devotionally are explained and exemplified by means of an extended story. The main characters in the story are Victoria, a new Christian in her mid-20s, and Sharon, a mother and a pastor's wife who is mentoring her. Each is blessed by discovering—or rediscovering—how to read the Bible devotionally, though for different reasons. You will be given a bird's-eye view of a long-term discipleship process, as well as the opportunity to listen in as each character meets God in Scripture. Other helpful Spiritual Formation practices, such as prayer, Scripture memorization, and overcoming temptation, will be modeled through story as well. My prayer is that you too might be inspired and instructed to encounter God daily in the pages of the Bible. The process is not difficult, but mastery is a journey of a lifetime. May God bless you, challenge you, and change you, as he meets you in his Word. Let's get back to our story.

Victoria's First Quiet Time

Because the rest of the week was so hectic, Victoria didn't have the opportunity to follow Sharon's advice until Saturday. Her body was used to getting up for work early, so she woke up at the usual time and couldn't get back to sleep. After fighting it for a while she reluctantly got out of bed, made some coffee in the French press (which was always the longest four minutes of her morning), took out her Bible, and sat down on the couch in the living room. Remembering what Sharon had told her, she prayed, "God, please meet me in your Word and give me the strength to change my life because of our meeting." She looked at the table of contents to find the Gospel of John (which was the last of the four Gospels in the New Testament, she observed), and began to read. "In the beginning was the Word, and the Word was with God, and the Word was God."[6] This was going to be interesting. As she read on, she worked out from the context that the Word was Jesus, and that the verse was saying that Jesus not only was with God from the beginning but was actually God himself.

Victoria quickly realized that if she was going to ask the three questions that Sharon recommended, she needed to figure out how much Scripture she should focus on during her Quiet Time. She wanted to keep the size of the passage relatively small so that she could read it several times and meditate on it, as Sharon had mentioned to her right before they left the coffee shop. Looking at the paragraphs in her Bible, she thought about reading just the first paragraph, but decided to include the second paragraph as well because the sentences were so short. In her Bible version those paragraphs contained eight verses.

> In the beginning was the Word, and the Word was with God, and the Word was God. He was in the beginning with God. All things were made through him, and without him was not any thing made that was made. In him was life, and the life was the light of men. The light shines in the darkness, and the darkness has not overcome it.
> There was a man sent from God, whose name was John. He came as a witness, to bear witness about the light, that all might believe through him. He was not the light, but came to bear witness about the light.[7]

She read the passage several times, first silently and then out loud, both because she was alone and because Sharon had told her that it was a good idea to involve several senses at the same time.

Then Victoria asked herself, "OK, what does this passage tell me about God?" She mentally answered herself. "It says that God and Jesus were the same. It says that the world was created through Jesus. It says that Jesus was both life and light, and that his light penetrated the darkness of the world. It also says that John was a witness to the light so that everyone would believe the truth about Jesus." She figured out by looking ahead a little bit that "John" referred to John the Baptist, not John the Gospel writer.

Her cell phone erupted in a ring tone, which startled her. "*Hola, mamá,*" she said as soon as she heard the voice at the other end. The flood of words overwhelmed her. Her mother was complaining again, about her father, about her brothers, and especially about her. The questions were always the same lately— why didn't she come over to the house more often? Why did she spend so much time at that church or with friends from that church? And why couldn't she find a nice boy at her mother's church? This last question was especially ironic because her mother had not attended her own church regularly for years. For her, church was a cultural thing, a family thing, not really a spiritual thing. It was hard for her to accept that Victoria had experienced something genuinely spiritual, both because it had never happened to her and because she thought it was taking her daughter away from her. Often Victoria felt torn between her new faith in Jesus and her desire to please her mother.

"*Mamá,*" Victoria interjected, hoping to keep the conversation from taking the turn that it had followed so many times in the past. "What if I come over and spend the day with you? I can help you clean the house, and then we can go shopping at the mall for those new shoes you've had your eyes on." The suggestion seemed to please her mother, and Victoria ended the call, cleaned up the kitchen hurriedly, and left the house.

Late that evening after she had returned home and taken a shower, Victoria picked up her Bible again and tried to resume her Quiet Time. Her brain was distracted from the events of the day and it took her some time to calm it down. Where did she leave off? "Lord, help me finish my Quiet Time tonight," was the prayer she shot off into the heavens; her friend Jennifer called them "arrow prayers." She seemed to remember some of her answers to the question about what the passage says about God, but didn't think that she had moved on to the next question yet. "I should have written this down in my notebook," she said to herself.

The second question that Sharon had recommended was, "What does this passage tell me about myself?" Victoria was stumped by this for a bit and reread the passage a couple of times, until it dawned on her that she could take the truths and images in the text and apply them to herself. Did she really believe that Jesus not only was God but that the world was created through him? Did her life reflect the light of Jesus more than the darkness of the world? And was she a witness to that light like John the Baptist was, so that other people could believe in Jesus because of what they saw in her? She suddenly realized that Jennifer had played that role in her own life, and had functioned as such a positive witness to Jesus over time that she had believed in Jesus herself. "God, thank you for the way that Jennifer was such a good witness," she silently prayed. "Please use me as a witness in someone else's life like you used Jennifer in my life."

She noticed that her prayer had just anticipated the final question: "With God's help, how should my life be changed so that I can become more like God, based on what I have learned both about God and about myself?" One answer to that question was that she should serve as a witness to others like John the Baptist and Jennifer had. But with a twinge of guilt she admitted that there were other ways in which her life needed to change, both to be more like the light of Jesus and to be a better witness to Jesus in the world. First among those ways was her language. Old habits die hard, and she struggled to purge from her speech the earthy and sometimes foul (she used to call them "colorful") words that she had used almost unconsciously for over a decade. Another was her tendency to gossip and to focus more on the faults of others than on resolving her own issues. Each of these were characteristics of which she was often largely unaware; she was only reminded of them when other people reflected them back to her, such as colleagues at work (generally somewhat snarkily) and her friend Jennifer (generally kindly).

The prayer that closed her first Quiet Time reflected what she had learned. "Dear God, thank you for teaching me about Jesus, and about John the Baptist and his witness to Jesus. Please give me the strength to control my language so that I can be a good witness to Jesus too, especially to Sofia at work who really needs your love right now since she has so many health and family problems. And please help me to stop gossiping, and instead to work on my own problems instead of focusing on other people's problems. Thank you for good friends like Jennifer, who knows who I really am and still loves me at the same time. Bless Sharon in the many things she does as a pastor's wife and a mother. And ..." Her voice caught in her throat. "And help my mom to understand that I have accepted Jesus as my Savior. Help her to come to know Jesus as her Savior too. In Jesus' name, Amen."

3

SHARON'S STORY

At the same time Victoria had finished making coffee and started her Quiet Time, Sharon had been up for almost two hours and washed two loads of laundry. A pastor's wife and a mother of three pleasantly rowdy kids rarely had time to sleep in, even on a weekend. She and her husband had an arrangement in which he was responsible for the kids on Saturday morning to give her some alone time, and in turn she corralled the kids on Sunday morning so that he could prepare for church. So here she was at the dining room table stirring half and half into her English Breakfast tea and reveling in the freedom, however temporary and constrained.

Events from the week bubbled up in her mind. She thought about a member of the congregation who had just been diagnosed with Stage IVB colon cancer. She thought about a parent-teacher conference where she discovered that her oldest son was doing poorly in two subjects, which was a complete surprise to her because he had conveniently forgotten to bring his report card home. And she thought about her meeting with Victoria and the Quiet Time advice she had given, which was ironic but fitting given her own experience.

Sharon had grown up in a Christian family as a middle child surrounded by boys; her mother had jokingly called her "a rose between two thorns." She accepted Christ as her Savior at a very young age, or so her parents said; she had no memory of the experience. To her it seemed as if she had grown up a believer, which was a source of pleasure to her but also a source of shame, since her greatest blessings occurred as a Christian but also her greatest sins. Bible knowledge was very important to the church her family attended, and Sharon excelled in memorizing not only the order of the books of the Bible but also large chunks of Scripture from all over the Bible. Throughout high school she was very active in church youth groups, even serving as a leader. She chose a Christian college, intending to major in Education and hoping to become a Christian Education Consultant for an international missions organization. But she met Josh at a class social during her junior year and within a month they were inseparable. They married right after graduation, and Sharon worked as an elementary school teacher to support her husband while he attended seminary to become a pastor.

In hindsight she realized that the seeds of her longtime spiritual struggle were sown in soil that many might wish they had in their own gardens. Her training in Bible knowledge as a child was a wonderful thing. Her assistance to her husband in his seminary course work was equally valuable, as was her ministry in the church when her husband graduated, became ordained, and took his first position as an assistant pastor. But several years as a pastor's wife, including numerous church crises, had confronted her with the reality that her faith had been far too superficial and based more on head knowledge than heart experience.

A voice interrupted her daydream. "Mom, where's my coat? Dad promised to take us out for breakfast." Her eldest son, forgetful as usual.

"It's in the back of the car, honey. Under the blanket, I think." Good. A bit more time to herself this morning. She resumed her train of thought.

The tipping point occurred when she was surprised to discover that her marriage was in trouble. Surely such a thing couldn't happen to *her*, could it? After all, she came from a long line of stable marriages, and she was a *pastor's* wife, for goodness sake! And yet it had. Josh had been spending more and more evenings on church-related business, which she increasingly resented. She too had become caught up in her own world, in women's ministries in the church and activities in her children's schools. And a long series of church squabbles, disagreements within the pastoral team, and staff discontent was taking its toll. All she could do was to cry out to a God whom she still knew with her head, but no longer with her heart.

Then a sweet saint with a gift of discernment approached her after church one Sunday, asked her how she was doing, and told her that she was praying for her. The dam broke, and all of the problems that had been building up for so long gushed out, as well as many tears. Doris asked about the state of her spiritual life (she used the words, "How is your walk with Jesus?") and did not seem surprised to discover that little actual walking with Jesus had occurred over the last few years. Gently and lovingly, Doris reminded Sharon about what she already knew but had not practiced as a habit, that time alone both with Jesus and with her spouse was vital not just for an effective ministry but also for a satisfying and fulfilled life. She painfully adjusted her schedule commitments one by one to make such a practice structurally possible, and relearned the benefits of having a regular encounter with God in his Word as a result. Thanks to Josh's mother, who was gratifyingly eager to watch the kids, Sharon and Josh were also able to enjoy date nights every other

Friday night. And gradually things had improved, in her marriage, in her family, and in her ministry.

4

SHARON'S QUIET TIME

She drained the last of the tea from her mug and prayed with her eyes open. "Lord, speak to me from your Word. I am your servant, and I am listening." She loved to echo those words of Samuel in the prayer that often began her Quiet Time.[8] Opening her Bible, Sharon turned the pages not to the beginning of the letter to the Philippians, as listed in her Bible reading plan, but instead to the end. Chapter 4 of Philippians, especially the sweet spot in the middle, was both familiar to her and much loved by her, and Sharon sensed that it was a passage she especially needed to hear right now. She and Josh had no idea when they were in seminary that one of the most difficult challenges of pastoral ministry—a challenge so daunting that many left the ministry within five years of graduation because of it—was handling personal attacks from members of the congregation. Attacks from those she had thought were her friends were especially devastating, like the Johnsons whom they had often invited into their home only to see them recently leave the church and complain bitterly to the Elders before they went. She was acutely aware that the unending politics of church leadership had worn her down and affected not only her emotions but also her thought process. In her raw weariness she returned from time to time to these words in Philippians, which she regarded as God's Prescription for Mental Health.

> Rejoice in the Lord always; again I will say, rejoice. Let your reasonableness be known to everyone. The Lord is at hand; do not be anxious about anything, but in everything by prayer and supplication with thanksgiving let your requests be made known to God. And the peace of God, which surpasses all understanding, will guard your hearts and your minds in Christ Jesus.
> Finally, brothers, whatever is true, whatever is honorable, whatever is just, whatever is pure, whatever is lovely, whatever is commendable, if there is any excellence, if there is anything worthy of praise, think about these things. What you have learned and received and heard and seen in me—practice these things, and the God of peace will be with you.[9]

She read this passage over and over, bathing in it, reveling in it, drinking it in like water to a thirsty soul. From her previous study of Philippians Sharon knew that the apostle Paul had written to the church in the city of Philippi while he was in jail, and that far from being a bitter or angry letter it was instead full of joy. Paul had obviously learned personally the lessons he was passing on to the church, perhaps *because* he had been thrown in jail. And the many exhortations to unity and humility, some of which were addressed to specific leaders in the church, seemed to indicate that the congregation in Philippi was no stranger to church leadership conflict either.

Because she had developed some expertise in having a Quiet Time, Sharon often liked to address several questions at once and to vary the order of the questions. This time she went straight to the application question. "With God's help, how should my life be changed so that I can become more like God? In other words, how does God want me to apply what I've learned in the text about God and about myself?" And this passage in Philippians 4 was so rich that it was fairly dripping with applications, especially given her current situation. "Rejoice in the Lord always"[10] was the command that began the passage. It was so important that Paul repeated it twice, and was an example of the theme of joy that Philippians was soaked in. Why should someone rejoice, even though the circumstances might be grim? Sharon was reminded of one of her favorite verses in the Bible, from the book of Romans: "And we know that for those who love God all things work together for good, for those who are called according to his purpose."[11] Surely *that* was a wonderful reason to rejoice: the sovereign control of God over the situations of life.

So how could she rejoice in her own situation? If she were honest with herself, there were actually *many* reasons to rejoice. She could rejoice that her church was larger, more diverse, and in a better building than when she and Josh had arrived several years ago. She could rejoice that her marriage was finally starting to get back on track, and that she was truly partnering with her husband in the work of the gospel. And she could rejoice that the church was making a concerted effort to reach out to the neighborhood and the larger community in her city, and that those efforts had been recognized not only by the local neighborhood association but also by a city counselor for the district.

Next command. "Let your reasonableness be known to everyone."[12] Sharon knew what "reasonableness" meant, of course, but was not quite sure why Paul would make that particular command right here. A marginal note on the word "reasonableness" in her Bible offered "gentleness" as an alternative. She quickly scanned another Bible translation that she had brought to the table and found the word "gentleness" there too. That made a bit more sense; maybe Paul was saying that in the midst of crises we should rejoice and be gentle and reasonable with one another, instead of harsh and contentious. And it struck her that if she ran into the Johnsons around town, which she was likely to do since they lived so close, God was telling her to be gentle and forgiving with them, not defensive and hurt.

"The Lord is at hand."[13] Did this mean that Jesus could return at any time, so we should live lives that are worthy of him? Possibly, but her other translation read "The Lord is near," so "at hand" could also mean "near" or "close." That interpretation seemed to fit better with the next verse. Instead of being anxious about anything we should pray and make our requests about everything to "The God Who Is Near." And we should do this with thanksgiving, because we know that God will answer our prayers.

Then came the precious promise of peace, the peace that surpasses all understanding because there is no logical reason why it should exist given the circumstances, the peace that will banish all anxiety and worry and will replace them with assurance that God is in control. That peace literally guards our hearts. Sharon couldn't help but think of Paul writing in his jail cell, and intentionally comparing the peace from God after prayer with the armed guard that probably stood watch outside his cell.

These were the words that Sharon needed to hear, and which soothed her soul. "Lord," she prayed. "You know how bothered and hurt I am by all the things that are happening at church right now. People leaving that we were close to, like the Johnsons. The disagreements among the Elders about the vision and direction of the church. The difficulty in attracting and retaining young families. The budget problems we've been having. Even the hard time getting people to teach Sunday School and to volunteer for the nursery. There are times when I just can't stop thinking about all these things, and it even wakes me up at night. Lord, I know that you are in control, and that I can trust you with *all* the details of our lives, the big ones and the small ones. Please resolve these problems, in ways that I'm sure I can't even imagine right now. Fulfill the desire you placed in our hearts for a growing, dynamic, healthy church that worships you together according to your Word and in the power of your Holy Spirit. And I claim the promise of peace that will guard my heart from the anxiety that I have just given to you, so that it doesn't keep returning. I pray this in the strong name of Jesus. Amen."

Sharon sat back, relieved and refreshed, not sure how God was going to answer her prayer but confident that he would. She heard the garage door open and car doors slam; the kids had come home from breakfast and her time alone was about to end. She noticed that the rest of the passage in her Quiet Time served as a follow-up to the prayer she had just prayed, and was designed to focus our minds properly so that the anxiety did not recur. In that sense this passage really *was* God's Prescription for Mental Health. Whatever is honorable, pure, lovely, and commendable, whatever is excellent and worthy of praise, choose to think on *those* things, not on the problems and issues that cause so much worry. You've given your problems to God in prayer; don't take them back.

Paul ended the passage with a command that again culminated in a promise of peace: "What you have learned and received and heard and seen in me—practice these things, and the God of peace will be with you."[14] For Sharon this was confirmation that Paul had learned personally the truths in his commands and had experienced the peace that came from them. But she was convinced that God was also telling *her* to follow the example of the apostle Paul. Just as Paul was holding himself up as a model for the church in Philippi to learn from, so too she should serve as a model of prayer and peace for her own church, including Victoria. In the few moments of solitude she had remaining she quickly prayed, "Lord, help me to focus on the beautiful things you have given me instead of the ugly things. And help me to be a good example of your love and grace to the church, especially to Victoria. Amen." The kitchen door opened and the weekend whirlwind began.

Bible Translations
and the ACTS Prayer

The following Tuesday evening Sharon and Victoria met at the coffee shop again. Josh watched the kids on Tuesday evenings too, so that Sharon could be involved in church ministry. Victoria seemed a bit subdued as she brought her coffee back to their table. "How have you been, Victoria?" asked Sharon.

Victoria looked close to tears. "It's my mom," she almost whispered. "The doctors found a lump, and she's going in to have it checked next week."

Sharon's heart melted. "Oh, Victoria, I'm so sorry to hear. Can we help her in any way, like providing rides to the doctor's office or bringing over food?"

"Thank you, Sharon. That's very kind of you. But I'm taking that day off so that I can drive her to the hospital and back, and then I'll probably stay overnight at her house to keep her company. My dad and my brothers, they don't look after her very well, and she keeps wanting me to move back home." Victoria tugged at her hair in nervousness and worry. "My mom also doesn't like the fact that I spend so much time in church, or at least not in the church I went to when I was a kid. She doesn't understand why I want to learn how to read the Bible and pray on my own. It's not the way she was raised. But my mom is so worried about her health right now that it would really help her if she could learn how to read the Bible and pray to Jesus too."

The two women talked some more about Victoria's mother and the kinds of things that could cause the lump that was found. Then Sharon reached out and touched Victoria's arm and said, "Can I pray for you and your mom?" Victoria nodded, and Sharon bowed her head.

"Heavenly Father, we lift up Victoria's mom to you right now and ask for wisdom for the doctors as they try to determine what the lump is and why it's there. In your grace and mercy, we ask that her condition not turn out to be a serious one, and that the uncertainty be resolved quickly. We also ask that you use this situation to draw Victoria's mom to you, so that she realizes that she needs you and accepts you as her Savior and Lord. I pray, too, that Victoria not be anxious or worried about anything, but would instead leave these requests at your feet and trust that you are a God who delights in answering the prayers of his people. And I claim the promise in Philippians 4 for Victoria, that your peace would guard her heart and mind in the truth about how much you love her and her mom. We pray these things in the name of your Son Jesus. Amen."

Sharon withdrew her hand. Victoria looked up briefly and said, "Thank you," then dropped her head again. Sharon tried to catch her eye and change the subject. "How did things go with your Quiet Times last week?" she asked.

"OK, I think," Victoria replied after a pause. "It was hard to find enough time to have a complete Quiet Time in one sitting. I often had to pick up where I left off the previous time. Am I doing it right, or should I pick shorter passages of Scripture so that I can finish sooner?"

"The same thing happens to me, too," Sharon assured her. "Yes, you can focus on smaller chunks of Scripture that you're able to work through in one sitting, like three to five verses for each ten- to fifteen-minute time block that you have. But don't worry if you have to pick up where you left off the next time. Life happens. God knows that."

Victoria looked relieved. "That's good to hear; I was hoping that was OK. Oh, two other things. Does it matter which version of the Bible I use? I've been using the one that Jennifer gave me, the one the church uses, the English Standard Version, I think. Is that what I should be reading? Or would something else be better for my Quiet Times?"

Sharon smiled; this was a common question from newcomers at church, and many people seemed to be more comfortable asking her this question instead of her husband for some reason. "The English Standard Version (we call it by its initials, the ESV) is a good choice; that's why our church uses it. But it never hurts to have a couple of others to choose from, either for variety or to refer to when you're confused by something in your main version. I like to keep a New International Version handy, the NIV, in case I'm not sure what the ESV means, or vice versa. Other good choices are the Christian Standard Bible—the CSB—and the New Living Translation, the NLT."

She paused for a moment to decide if she wanted to say more. "One thing to keep in mind is that translations fall along a spectrum from being very literal, to balanced, to relatively free when it comes to their translation style. What that means is the degree to which a translation follows the phrasing and word order of the Greek and Hebrew languages in which the Bible was originally written. For example, the New American Standard Bible is at the literal end of that spectrum, and The Message is at the free or paraphrase end. If you can, try to pick versions from different parts of that spectrum so that you can compare them with each other if the passage you are reading seems a bit confusing. I like to keep three or four around to bounce off each other if I get stuck—the ESV, the NIV, the NLT, and sometimes the CSB. But if you had to pick only two, the ESV and the NIV complement each other pretty well."

"The only one I have is an ESV," said Victoria. "Or at least that's the only one I actually use; I have a Bible that was given to me at church when I was a kid, but from what I remember it was pretty hard to understand."

"Let me get you an NIV," Sharon offered. "We have a couple of extra ones at home. However, there are a whole lot of other useful translations out there. For example, Josh likes to keep a NET Bible handy, the New English Translation, mostly because of the informative study notes about the original Greek or Hebrew. My mother prefers the Revised New Jerusalem Bible because it sounds so good when read aloud. And for dignity and sheer history, you can't beat the King James Version, although it can also sound strange at times." She looked down at her phone. "Many of the translations I've mentioned have free apps that you can get for your phone or tablet. Before we go, I can show you the ones I have on my phone, if you'd like."

"Thank you; I *would* like that. And thank you for your offer of an NIV." Victoria bit her lip and thought for a second. "Oh, yeah, I almost forgot. How should I pray during my Quiet Time? I know that prayer is just talking with God. But should I be talking with him in any special way when I read the Bible?"

"That's a *great* question, Victoria. Prayer is just talking with God, to be sure; but it is also a lifelong journey. We are constantly learning how to pray differently, more deeply, more wisely, more intimately. Let me suggest a couple of things, first about prayer in general, and then about prayer during a Quiet Time. Did Jennifer ever tell you about ACTS Prayer?"

Victoria shook her head. "I don't think so. What's that?"

"ACTS is just an acronym for structuring your prayer time around four kinds of prayer. The 'A' stands for Adoration, the 'C' for Confession, the 'T' for Thanksgiving, and the 'S' for Supplication, which just means asking God for something. Most of the components of an ACTS Prayer are found in the Lord's Prayer, which is the model prayer that Jesus taught his disciples to pray.[15] I think the ACTS way of organizing prayer came about because our prayers can tend to be unbalanced and tilted toward asking God for things instead of praising him or thanking him. In ACTS Prayer the requests occur at the end instead of dominating the whole prayer time."

"So ACTS Prayer is just prayer in which you do 'A' first, then 'C,' then 'T,' then 'S'?"

"Right. ACTS Prayer is really pretty simple. First you adore God in prayer, which means praising him for who he is, our powerful Creator God. If you get stuck, pull out pretty much any psalm to serve as an example. The ones at the end of the book of Psalms, numbers 146 through 150, are particularly good models. Focusing on who God is can't help but shine a light on who *we* are by comparison, which leads to confession because our sin falls so short of the high standard set by a holy God. A great example of confession is Psalm 51, the psalm that King David wrote after the prophet Nathan called him out because of his adultery with Bathsheba."

Victoria scrunched up her face in puzzlement. Sharon asked, "Do you remember that story, about King David and Bathsheba and her husband, Uriah the Hittite?"

"I'm not sure. Could you remind me?"

Sharon spent a few minutes telling her the story from 2 Samuel about David's adultery with Bathsheba, his complicity in the death of her husband, the accusations of Nathan the prophet,

David's realization and confession of sin, the death of the firstborn son of David and Bathsheba, and the birth of their second son Solomon.[16] She also explained that Psalm 51 was written out of that experience of horrible sin, heartfelt confession, and wonderful forgiveness.

Sharon resumed her discussion of the ACTS Prayer outline. "One of the most precious verses in Psalm 51 is verse 10, where David says, 'Create in me a clean heart, O God, and renew a right spirit within me.'[17] That can be a great verse to use either to transition into or transition out of the confession portion of an ACTS Prayer."

"So that's the letter 'C,' right, in ACTS? And 'T' is Thanksgiving?"

"Exactly. In an ACTS Prayer, confession moves directly into thanksgiving, both because of the incredible forgiveness that God has granted us in *particular* when we confess our sins, and because of all of the wonderful things that God has done for us in *general*. Psalm 106 is a great example of the first kind of thanksgiving, meaning thanksgiving for how God has forgiven us in particular. The author thanks God at the beginning of the psalm for his goodness, but the rest of the psalm reviews the history of Israel to indicate *why* in particular the psalmist was thanking him: because of God's forgiveness and faithfulness despite the frequent idolatry and unfaithfulness of Israel. Psalm 138 is an example of the second kind of thanksgiving, meaning thanksgiving for what God has done for us in general. You may want to take a look at those two psalms when you get home. They're both good models of thanksgiving."

Sharon took a sip of her tea. Victoria was looking at her attentively, as if she was eager for her to finish the explanation of ACTS Prayer. All of this was new to Victoria; Jennifer had told her about short, immediate "arrow" prayers to God, and she knew about the Lord's Prayer because of the times they recited it in church. But she had very little experience with other ways of praying, and if truth be told she spent far more time thinking about God than actually talking to God.

A few drops of tea had spilled on the table, so Sharon dabbed her napkin at them. "The last letter in ACTS stands for Supplication, which is the thing that tends to dominate our prayers unless we make a conscious effort otherwise. That's where the ACTS outline is so helpful, because it provides balance in prayer. But even our requests need to be balanced so that they aren't self-centered and materialistic all of the time. You know what I mean, the 'gimme gimme' kind of prayer? 'God give me this, God give me that'?"

Victoria nodded her head, because she knew *exactly* what Sharon meant. Sometimes she thought that the little bit of prayer she actually did was almost entirely about asking God to give her things. And to give things to her mom, of course.

Sharon finished her cup of now-cold tea and grimaced as the bitter leaf particles at the bottom slid down her throat. "In several of his letters, the apostle Paul included both a thanksgiving and a prayer for the church that he was writing to. These thanksgivings and prayers usually occurred right at the beginning of the letter. The wonderful thing about those thanksgivings and prayers is that they are both specific and general at the same time. In other words, they are addressed to the needs of the particular church he was talking to, but sufficiently general that they are also applicable to the Church throughout the ages. Because of this, they can serve as excellent models for our own thanksgiving and supplication prayers in the ACTS Prayer outline. Let me give you an example from the letter to the Philippians, which is one of my favorite books of the Bible because it has been so helpful to me. I'll read it to you; if you want to follow along, it's in Philippians 1, verses 3 through 11."

Sharon tapped on the screen of the Bible app on her phone, got derailed for a second because she hit Ephesians instead of Philippians, and began to read.

> I thank my God in all my remembrance of you, always in every prayer of mine for you all making my prayer with joy, because of your partnership in the gospel from the first day until now. And I am sure of this, that he who began a good work in you will bring it to completion at the day of Jesus Christ. It is right for me to feel this way about you all, because I hold you in my heart, for you are all partakers with me of grace, both in my imprisonment and in the defense and confirmation of the gospel. For God is my witness, how I yearn for you all with the affection of Christ Jesus. And it is my prayer that your love may abound more and more, with knowledge and all discernment, so that you may approve what is excellent, and so be pure and blameless for the day of Christ, filled with the fruit of righteousness that comes through Jesus Christ, to the glory and praise of God.[18]

Since her throat felt a bit dry, Sharon glanced up at the menu board in the coffee shop to see if she wanted to order anything else. She was constantly amazed that almost everything on the board cost several dollars, so she decided against it. Besides, the giving at church had been on a downward trend for the last several months, so she and Josh were tightening the belt of their family budget just in case they were asked to take another salary freeze by the Board of Elders. "This passage is a great one to take a look at because you can almost consider it a package of the last two kinds of prayer in the ACTS outline, a Thanksgiving followed by a Supplication. And look at the details of what Paul *thanks* God for, and then what he *asks* God for. He starts out by saying that he thanks God 'in all my remembrance of you.'[19] Josh says that in the original, that means something like 'I pray for you whenever you come to my mind.' Isn't that a great way to pray for somebody regularly? Whenever you think about them?"

Victoria nodded her head in agreement. "Yeah, too often I find myself saying to someone, 'I'll be praying for you,' or, 'You'll be in my thoughts and prayers,' when they're really not. Maybe what I can do instead is to actually pray for them whenever I think about them."

"Right, especially because it's entirely possible that it was God who brought them to your mind in the first place, so that you *could* pray for them. I'm convinced that that's how our God works. Not only does he answer the prayers of his people, but he also motivates and enables them to pray to begin with. Life really *is* 'All God All The Time,' from beginning to end."

All of a sudden Sharon became aware of the passage of time, and looked at her watch. "I'm so sorry, Victoria; I've really enjoyed our discussion, but time has gotten away from me and I need to get home to put the kids to bed. We can pick up where we left off the next time we get together. In the meantime, maybe you could try *starting* your Quiet Times with the Adoration and Confession parts of an ACTS Prayer, and *ending* your Quiet Times with the Thanksgiving and Supplication parts based on what God has told you *during* your Quiet Time. Does that make sense?"

"It does. Thanks."

"Could you close us with prayer tonight?"

"Sure!" Victoria bowed her head and thanked God for their time together. She also asked God for her mom's lump to be benign, and to give Sharon energy for all of her family and ministry responsibilities. After she said "Amen," the two women stood up, hugged each other, cleared off the table, and left the coffee shop.

6

Victoria's Quiet Time
Using an ACTS Prayer

A couple of nights later Victoria finally was able to slow down and have a Quiet Time. She was exhausted, both physically and emotionally, because of the hectic pace at work and the health situation with her mother. As she collapsed on the couch, she tried to remember what Sharon had told her the other night at the coffee shop. "Oh yeah," she said to herself. "I need to start with the first two parts of an ACTS Prayer and end with the last two parts." She closed her eyes and began to pray.

"God, I'm not quite sure how I should adore you in prayer. Thank you for coming into my heart and changing my life."

"Wait," she thought. "That's a thanksgiving. I'm not supposed to do that until the end, right? It probably doesn't matter. But how do I adore God in prayer?"

She opened her eyes. As she looked for her Bible, she remembered what Sharon had texted her in reply when she had asked a question about ACTS Prayer. She said that you adored God for who he *is* but thanked him for what he has *done*. Since Sharon had recommended the last few psalms as examples of adoration,

Victoria went straight to the very end of the book, hoping that Psalm 150 was as good an example as any.

> Praise the Lord!
> Praise God in his sanctuary;
>   praise him in his mighty heavens!
> Praise him for his mighty deeds;
>   praise him according to his excellent greatness!
> Praise him with trumpet sound;
>   praise him with lute and harp!
> Praise him with tambourine and dance;
>   praise him with strings and pipe!
> Praise him with sounding cymbals;
>   praise him with loud clashing cymbals!
> Let everything that has breath praise the Lord!
>   Praise the Lord![20]

She couldn't quite decide whether the praise in this psalm was an example of adoration or thanksgiving; it seemed to be a mixture of both. But with Psalm 150 before her, she resumed her prayer. "God, I adore you because you are the Creator of the world. I adore you together with all your people. I adore you both for who you are and for what you have done. I adore you loud and proud. And not only do your people adore you, but everything that you have made adores you."

Victoria stopped, because she knew what was coming next. Confession always made her uncomfortable, even when she was alone with God. And sometimes, like this evening, she had a lot to confess. She took a deep breath and plunged in.

"God, I'm sorry for going off on Belinda today at work. She makes me so mad! Always ordering people around even though she's not the boss. But I shouldn't have spoken to her that way, especially using the words that I did. I simply can't imagine trying to share my faith with her right now; what would she think? Would she even *want* to be a Christian if she thought I was a typical example? Anyway, please help me to watch my mouth. Please work in Belinda's life too, and make her less bossy. Even though I've probably been a lousy witness, please help her come to know you as her Savior. Please don't let me blow my witness with Sofía, who needs you in her life really badly right now. And please keep me from worrying so much about my mom. Help me to trust that you are in control of everything and that everything that happens is intended for our good. Amen."

Victoria was aware that her opening prayer ended up with some supplications in it, but at least it was more balanced than most of her prayers tended to be. On to the Quiet Time. She had already picked the passage she wanted to read. Her friend Jennifer had recommended it to her because she knew that Victoria was so anxious about her mother's health. "Psalm 23 is one of my favorite psalms when I'm worried and need comfort," Jennifer had said. "It's a pretty famous one, too." Victoria turned back a little in her Bible and found Psalm 23.

> The Lord is my shepherd; I shall not want.
> > He makes me lie down in green pastures.
> He leads me beside still waters.
> > He restores my soul.
> He leads me in paths of righteousness
> > for his name's sake.
> Even though I walk through the valley
> > of the shadow of death,
> > I will fear no evil,
> for you are with me;
> > your rod and your staff,

they comfort me.
You prepare a table before me
    in the presence of my enemies;
you anoint my head with oil;
    my cup overflows.
Surely goodness and mercy shall follow me
    all the days of my life,
and I shall dwell in the house of the Lord
    forever.[21]

Victoria read it through several times and could feel peace washing over her. No wonder the psalm was so well-known. "Let's see; what does this psalm tell me about God?" she asked herself. "It says that God is a shepherd who cares for every need of his sheep and leads his sheep in the direction of things that are good for them. He comforts and protects his sheep in times of danger. Not only does he provide for their basic needs but he also blesses them publicly in front of enemies who want to take the blessing away. Because of God's care for them, sheep who follow God as their shepherd enjoy goodness, mercy, and security for their entire life."

"So far so good," she thought. "What does this psalm tell me about myself? It tells me that I am a sheep who needs to follow the lead of God as my shepherd, and who needs to trust him to comfort me, protect me, and provide for me." Her mind leaped ahead to the final question. "With God's help, how should my life be changed so that I can become more like God?" She reviewed the psalm for a minute or two. "Well, what *I* need to do to become that person in the psalm, that sheep who calmly trusts God, is to really live out that trust when times get rough, instead of just talking trust. I need to have faith that my mom is in God's hands instead of obsessing about her health and worrying about her constantly.

I need to relax when people bother me at work, and trust that in the end God will defend me so that I'm not always thinking I have to defend myself. Above all, I need to truly believe in God's goodness and mercy instead of being consumed by fear and anxiety. And I need God's help for all these things because I can't do them by myself."

Victoria yawned a little and looked at the clock. Time for bed; it had been a tough day, but this was a nice way to end it. She had noticed that a Quiet Time and prayer before bed often prepared her for a night of undisturbed sleep. "OK, let me end with the 'T' and 'S' parts of the prayer," she said to herself. "God, I thank you for what you have shown me in this psalm, that you are a gentle shepherd who cares for me and protects me and wants to comfort me. Please help me to trust that you care for my mom too, and please keep her lump from being cancerous. And help me either to keep my mouth shut at work when I feel provoked, or to say gentle words to make the situation better instead of harsh words to make the situation worse. In Jesus' name, Amen." With that, she switched out the lights and went into her bedroom.

7

BIBLE READING PLANS

Their Tuesday evening meeting was cancelled for a couple of weeks because of sickness that swept through Sharon's family, starting with the kids, then the parents, and back again. As she drove to the coffee shop, Sharon mused that children at school were little human Petri dishes, compact breeding grounds for the cultivation and transmission of germs. She had wanted to shelter Victoria from the bug that her family had caught, but now that it had run its course, she missed their time together and knew they had a lot to catch up on.

Victoria was waiting for her at their usual table. She often got there early to grab that private spot in the corner. Sometimes they found the table already occupied, which always threw off their rhythm for a few minutes as they tried to find another acceptable table and reestablish their routine in the new location. Sharon reflected wryly that the same thing happens at church when other people sit in what have habitually become "your" seats; it throws off your routine and makes a surprising amount of the rest of the worship service seem strange and annoying. People were such creatures of habit.

The two women hugged each other and Sharon went to the counter to order. When she returned, Sharon asked Victoria how her mom was doing. Victoria brought her up to date, and the tears that were never far from the surface overflowed and started running down her face. Victoria wiped them away with a tissue and looked around self-consciously.

They talked about her mom some more, then her job, and then Sharon's family. Finally, Sharon asked, "How's your Quiet Time going, Victoria?"

"I think it's going pretty well," Victoria replied. "I mean, it's hard to have one every day, or at least every day at the same time. And I think I'm getting the hang of the ACTS Prayer. You want me to do the 'AC' part *before* the Quiet Time and the 'TS' part *after* the Quiet Time, right?"

"Yes, that was just a suggestion about how you could apply the ACTS Prayer model to a Quiet Time. The 'AC' part could help prepare you for the Quiet Time, and the 'TS' part could bring the Quiet Time to an end by thanking God for what you have learned and asking for his help to put it into practice. That's a good time to pray for other people as well."

"Then why isn't it called the 'AC Prayer' and the 'TS Prayer'? Why the 'ACTS Prayer'?"

"Well, the ACTS Prayer is a prayer outline that you hear about a lot. It really applies to an *entire* prayer session, when all you are focusing on is prayer. It was designed to make prayer more balanced, so that you're not spending the entire time asking God for things. And the ACTS acronym is easy to remember. I've just adapted it for a Quiet Time setting, so that 'AC' sets you up for the Quiet Time, and 'TS' finishes off the Quiet Time by taking the results of the Quiet Time and turning them into prayer."

"Ah, that makes sense. And that's how I've been doing it."

"But there are *other* ways to do it," Sharon continued. "One way is to pick a Bible verse to use as a prayer to start your Quiet Time. There's a verse in the Psalms that is great for this; Josh often uses it as a prayer before he preaches. Let me see if I can find it." Sharon had already logged into the Wi-Fi at the coffee shop, so she did an Internet search for the verse. "Here it is: Psalm 19, verse 14."

> Let the words of my mouth and the meditation of my heart
> be acceptable in your sight,
> O Lord, my rock and my redeemer.[22]

"So you could pray that verse at the beginning of your Quiet Time as a way to prepare your heart. Another good verse comes from Psalm 51, the psalm about confession that I mentioned to you before. That one is pretty easy to find." She tapped a few times on the Bible app on her phone.

> Create in me a clean heart, O God,
> and renew a right spirit within me.[23]

"That's verse 10 in Psalm 51. It helps prepare you for a Quiet Time by starting with confession, which might be particularly important on certain days." Sharon stopped to allow other verses to come to mind, then decided that she had already provided a good starting point. "You can also end with a Scripture verse, but I generally prefer to make my closing prayer reflect the results of my Quiet Time, like thanking God for what he has shown me and asking for his strength to put it into practice. But if you *wanted* to end with a Scripture verse, this one might be a good one." Two taps later she began to read:

The Lord is my portion;
> I promise to keep your words.
I entreat your favor with all my heart;
> be gracious to me according to your promise.
When I think on my ways,
> I turn my feet to your testimonies;
I hasten and do not delay
> to keep your commandments.[24]

"OK, that was actually *several* verses," Sharon said quickly. "It's from Psalm 119, verses 57 through 60. That passage is all about obedience, and a great way to end your Quiet Time is on a note of obedience to what you have just learned. Besides, Psalm 119 is a wonderful psalm whose entire theme is the Word of God, so if you study it you can probably find several good verses to use to begin and end your Quiet Times."

As Sharon was speaking, Victoria was writing everything down in her little spiral notebook. When Sharon had finished, Victoria was reminded that she should be writing things down during her Quiet Times too. And that she had other things to ask Sharon about this evening.

Victoria put down her pen. "I've got a question. You told me to start with the Gospel of John, and I've mostly been doing that. Except when I really needed to read something helpful for what I've been going through, like Psalm 23 or other passages that Jennifer has recommended to me. But is there some kind of reading plan that I should be following for my Quiet Time? I mean, what do I read when I'm done with the Gospel of John?"

Sharon responded with a smile. "There are a *lot* of answers to that question, especially these days. Let's see if we can find one that fits you. The first thing to mention is that reading the Bible and having a Quiet Time are actually two different things. They're related, of course, and you can't have a real Quiet Time without reading the Bible. But in general, one of the main reasons to read the Bible, especially by using a reading plan, is to *learn* about the Bible and the God of the Bible. By contrast, the purpose of a Quiet Time is to *meet* God in the Bible."

Victoria frowned. "I'm confused. I thought the main reason you read the Bible is to meet God."

Remembering when she had thought the same thing, and the way her experience had drifted over time, Sharon put her hand on Victoria's arm. "That's a great way to look at it. And I hope that's *always* the way it is for you. But in practice, there's something that can happen that you would be wise to guard against. Especially if you're a new believer, there's so much to learn that it's easy to get so caught up in reading the Bible to learn about the *Bible*, or even the *God* of the Bible, that you forget to actually *meet* God in the Bible. The Bible then becomes something for the head instead of something for the heart. I've told you a little about this before, but that's exactly what happened to me. When Josh went to seminary, we both got so absorbed in all of the new things that he was learning about the Bible and the Christian faith that over time we drifted away from the main purpose of the Bible, which is to tell us about God so that we can have a better relationship with him. And then Josh graduated and got his first job as a pastor, and the constant demands of ministry made things worse. I just don't want you to make the same mistakes that I did."

"So how do I keep from doing that?"

"Here's one thing I would recommend. Think of a Bible reading plan and your Quiet Time as two separate but related things. Ideally, your Quiet Time should build upon something you have read in your reading plan. It is a *really* good idea to read your Bible regularly, even daily if you can, and to read it through cover to cover. What many people try to do is to read the Bible through every year. At least, that's what they say in January when they are making their New Year's resolutions. By March most people have fallen by the wayside. But it's still a good goal to set for yourself."

Sharon paused, because she wasn't sure she was as clear as she should have been. "Let me get really specific. Let's say you are following a one-year reading plan. In practical terms, it can take anywhere from 15 to 30 minutes to do your daily reading assignment, especially if you're reading a very long chapter or are stuck in one of those places in the Old Testament that consists of lists of names that never end. That's just the reading and learning part; now you need to have a Quiet Time too, so that you can meet God through what you have just read. Here's the thing: in order to finish your reading assignment, you need to read relatively quickly. But for a Quiet Time, you need to read a passage really *slowly*, and several times instead of just once. So I don't think you can do both at the same time. At least, *I* can't. What *I* have to do is to read my assignment, and then come back later and have a Quiet Time in a small passage inside that assignment that spoke to me as I was reading it, or which grew on me as I thought about it during the day. Even though I don't *always* do it this way, what works best for me is this: I do my reading assignment in the morning when I am fresh, and then I come back in the evening and have my Quiet Time in a short passage in that assignment when I am more relaxed and reflective."

She took a sip of her tea, which had gone cold. Too bad the coffee shop didn't have a microwave she could use to warm it up, or ceramic cups like traditional coffee shops had. Everything these days seemed to be designed for convenience and intended for the landfill. "Of course, I'm also more tired at night. But if I can actually schedule it, this seems to be the best combination for me. What you need to discover is what works best for *you*. It may not be the same thing each day. And you might even need to *alternate* your reading plan days and your Quiet Time days."

"I think I understand," Victoria replied tentatively. "I've pretty much been making my Quiet Time my reading plan. I've enjoyed it, but it's taking me a long time to get through the Gospel of John. And there's so much of the Bible left to go."

Sharon nodded her head vigorously in agreement. "Maybe the best way to think about it is that it's the work of a lifetime. That lets you relax a bit because you don't have to do it all at once. But there are ways you can be intentional about your reading of Scripture so that you can make good use of your time."

She looked at the clock on her phone. "Speaking of time, we're getting a bit short on it, so let's dive in. You can find a *lot* of one-year Bible reading plans on the Web. The one that is perhaps the best known was done a long time ago by Robert Murray M'Cheyne, who was a Scottish preacher in the 1800s. Try to find a one-page version that you can stick on your refrigerator; I'll send you a link to one when I get home. He divides daily readings into a family half and a personal or private half, but in your case just do them both yourself. Four passages are read every day, generally a single chapter each, from different books of the Bible. At the end of the year you will have finished the entire Bible once, and the New Testament and Psalms twice."

Sharon studied Victoria's face to make sure she still had her attention. "Some people find it more convenient to use an actual One Year Bible instead of just a reading list. You can find One Year Bibles in many popular translations, including the ESV and NIV. Those are organized a bit differently; you're still reading four passages every day, but they're from the Old Testament, the New Testament, the Psalms, and the book of Proverbs."

She held up her phone to show Victoria some app icons. "Of course, there's an app for that too. A lot of them, in fact. Some apps just give you reading lists to follow each day. Other apps include the biblical text for the day, and a few of them will actually *read* the text for you so that you can listen to it instead of reading it yourself. Many of those audio versions are straight readings of the text. But others actually *perform* those readings for you as if you were listening to a drama. And the great thing about these apps is that almost all of them are free. Some of them charge a small amount of money for certain Bible versions. But most of them are *completely* free. They're created by organizations that are doing this as a ministry, so donations are always welcome. Just something to keep in mind."

Sharon clicked on one of the app icons on her phone to show Victoria. "See, here's one. This one lets you choose from a *lot* of different reading plans, not just a single one like M'Cheyne's. It also keeps track of where you are in your reading plan, and will notify you if you are getting behind. You can even read through the same plan with other people."

Victoria put down her pen and shook her wrist a few times to keep her hand from cramping. "Wow, I had no idea that there were so many options. Where do you think I should begin?"

Sharon pursed her lips and looked up at the ceiling. "Well, the cheapest and least technology-intensive option might be the M'Cheyne reading plan. When you get the link that I'll send you later on this evening, you'll find that it is really easy to follow, basically four chapters a day. Some of the chapters can be pretty long, though, and can take some time to get through. That's why I recommend that you separate your reading plan from your Quiet Time and try to have your Quiet Time in a portion of one of the chapters in your reading plan. And when things get really busy, there's nothing wrong with doing your reading plan one day and your Quiet Time the next day. Of course, that would then mean that you would have a *two*-year reading plan, but at least you'd be in the Word every day."

She remembered something she forgot to mention. "There's actually a really simple way to read through the Bible without needing any lists or apps. If you read three chapters a day and five chapters on Sundays, you will get through the entire Bible in a year. If you have the time and are feeling ambitious, three chapters a day in the Old Testament and three chapters a day in the New Testament will get you through the Old Testament once and the New Testament *four* times in a year. But don't underestimate the time that this last approach will require every day."

A glance at her phone indicated that it was time to go. Sharon said a quick prayer for them both, then hugged Victoria and walked her out to her car. On the way home Sharon prayed that God would give Victoria the wisdom and perseverance both to read the Bible to get to know God, and to let the Bible read her so that she could get to know herself. She also prayed that Victoria's mind and heart would be fed and that her hands would obey what she had learned.

Memorizing Scripture

The next morning after the kids had gone off to school, Sharon had about a half an hour before she was due at church for a quilting group meeting. She couldn't quite make up her mind whether that was enough for a Quiet Time, so she asked God which passage she should pick, whether the next one on her reading plan or something else. Because she had found the passage in Philippians 4 so helpful, and because she realized that she had turned to it again and again during her Quiet Times over the last few months, Sharon felt that God was leading her to use her time to *memorize* the entire passage instead. She loved the Bible promise that hiding God's Word in her heart would protect the holiness of her heart.[25]

Sharon had participated in enough Bible memory competitions in Sunday School programs as a child that she understood the mechanics of memorization quite well. Verse by verse, clause by clause, break the passage down into pieces and memorize each piece, through observation, repetition, mental images, or association with rhythm or song. Then put the pieces back together again until more and more chunks of text were stored in your brain for the Holy Spirit to bring back to your mind just when you needed it, in his role as Counselor and Reminder.[26] Maybe she could use the next half hour to start the memorization process.

In her Bible, Philippians 4:4-9 consisted of two paragraphs, so the first breakdown was easy—memorize each paragraph separately, then put them together. Sharon reread the passage several times and observed something that she hoped might serve as a memory aid: the first paragraph contained *four* verses and consisted of *four* commands and a promise, while the second paragraph contained *two* verses and consisted of *two* commands and a promise. The strategy that had worked for her in the past was to memorize the first verse, then add the second verse to it, and so on, until the entire paragraph was committed to memory. In this case she thought she might be able to memorize two verses at once because she picked up several details that could help them stick in her mind. For example, the first verse repeated the command to rejoice twice; the second verse spoke of reasonableness, which began with the letter "r" just like rejoice; and the second half of the second verse spoke of "the Lord" just like the first half of the first verse. She even crafted a semi-rhythmic phrase to summarize the two verses and use as a mnemonic device: "Rejoicing is reason'ble 'cuz the Lord is at hand."

Her oldest son had excelled at Bible memorization in Sunday School largely by inventing songs that fit the words of the passage. Her middle child would create a rhythm that she would apply to the verses to help her remember them. And a close friend of Sharon's created mental pictures to guide the retrieval process. However, Sharon wasn't particularly musical or rhythmic, so she led with her strengths and went with what had always worked for her before. She was inspired by Josh's stories about a senior staff member at the Christian summer camp at which he had worked as a teenager. That staff member memorized entire books of the Bible simply by brute force repetition as he drove to work each day in bumper-to-bumper traffic.

After about 10 minutes of practice Sharon was able to repeat the first two verses by memory smoothly, without having to pause to grope for words in her mind. She looked at her watch; could she add any other verses before she had to leave? Verses 6 and 7 were a sweet spot that she had half memorized anyway. Negative command: don't be anxious. Positive command: let your requests be made known to God. How? By prayer and supplication with thanksgiving. Promise: the peace of God would guard your hearts and minds. What is that peace like? It surpasses all understanding.

She glanced at her watch again; time to go. She'd have to leave the full memorization of those verses for another day. However, she was encouraged by her progress. Sharon calculated that if she added only a single verse to her memory bank each day, then spent a day or two practicing the whole thing, she could commit the entire passage to long-term memory in about five days, maybe a week at the most. "Lord, give me the time and the discipline to hide this wonderful passage in my heart, and bring it back to my mind when I need it most," she prayed as she got up to leave.

9

SPIRITUAL JOURNALING

"Well, I think it might be time to learn another way to have a Quiet Time," Sharon led off after they got their drinks at the counter and found their table in the coffee shop. "Spiritual Journaling is another approach to reading the Bible devotionally so that you can meet God in Scripture. One type of Spiritual Journaling simply involves writing each of the steps of your Quiet Time down in a notebook. Some people do this after their Quiet Time has finished. But others do so as they go along, so that the very act of writing things down in a journal becomes the way that they discover what Scripture says and how God is speaking to them. You've mentioned yourself from time to time that you wished you wrote things down in a notebook while you were having your Quiet Time."

Victoria nodded. "For some reason I use my notebook more when I'm with you than when I'm alone having a Quiet Time. I need to remind myself to use it during my Quiet Times too."

"I understand. I don't do journaling much myself, but a lot of people find it helpful. Some people go all out with their journals, and fill them with poetry and stories and songs and drawings that are in some way inspired by the passage of Scripture that they are reading. They buy beautiful, blank journals with very artistic covers and write amazing things inside. Other people combine a Spiritual Journal with a Prayer Journal, which records prayer requests and answers to prayer over time. But what's interesting to me is that a particular *method* of having a Quiet Time has become associated with Spiritual Journaling. That method is called SOAP, for Scripture, Observation, Application, and Prayer. We've been doing each of these things already during our Quiet Times, just not under those names or necessarily in that order. But the SOAP method organizes a Quiet Time around those four steps and records the results of each step in a journal. It's really that simple."

"Huh," replied Victoria. "And I'd imagine that using the acronym SOAP makes each of the steps easy to remember, so you always know exactly what to do next."

SOAP Method of Spiritual Journaling

Scripture
Write down either the reference to the Scripture passage or the entire text of the Scripture passage.

Observation
Write down what you observe in the passage and how God is speaking to you from the passage.

Application
Write down how you plan to obey and apply what God is speaking to you from the passage.

Prayer
Write down a prayer based on the passage, perhaps using the ACTS Prayer outline (Adoration, Confession, Thanksgiving, Supplication).

Outline of the SOAP Method of Spiritual Journaling

"Right," agreed Sharon. "So what I was hoping we'd do this evening is to learn Spiritual Journaling by doing it together. We can use a passage of Scripture that addresses a couple of questions you've been asking. Remember when you texted me and asked for ways to handle temptation better? I thought we might look at a passage in the Gospel of Matthew that shows how Jesus *himself* handled temptation. I brought a notebook with me—nothing fancy, as you can see—that we can write in together in the SOAP format. Sound good?"

"Sure, sounds good. When I was younger, I kept a journal that started out like a diary but which ended up being a lot *more* than a diary. I wrote poetry in it and short stories in it as well as, you know, all my crushes on boys and my fights with girls and my frustrations with my parents. Typical teenage stuff. It had a little lock on it and I kept it under my bed so that nobody could find it."

"I know what you mean. And for many people, their journal does indeed function as a spiritual diary. Famous Christians throughout history have kept spiritual diaries, and some have been published and are very inspiring today. However, what we'll be talking about tonight is more of a specialized spiritual diary organized around reading the Bible devotionally using the SOAP method. I'm going to start by writing today's date in the notebook, and then the first heading, 'Scripture.' The passage I'd like to focus on comes from the first part of Matthew chapter 4. Let me find it and read it for you." Sharon tapped on her phone, brought the passage up on her screen, and began to read.

> Then Jesus was led up by the Spirit into the wilderness to be tempted by the devil. And after fasting forty days and forty nights, he was hungry. And the tempter came and said to him, "If you are the Son of God, command these stones to become loaves of bread." But he answered, "It is written,

> "'Man shall not live by bread alone,
> but by every word that comes from the mouth of God.'"

Then the devil took him to the holy city and set him on the pinnacle of the temple and said to him, "If you are the Son of God, throw yourself down, for it is written,

> "'He will command his angels concerning you,'

and

> "'On their hands they will bear you up,
> lest you strike your foot against a stone.'"

Jesus said to him, "Again it is written, 'You shall not put the Lord your God to the test.'" Again, the devil took him to a very high mountain and showed him all the kingdoms of the world and their glory. And he said to him, "All these I will give you, if you will fall down and worship me." Then Jesus said to him, "Be gone, Satan! For it is written,

> "'You shall worship the Lord your God
> and him only shall you serve.'"

Then the devil left him, and behold, angels came and were ministering to him.[27]

Victoria was following along on her own phone as Sharon was reading and looked up at her when she finished. "So does the Scripture step in SOAP mean that we should write down what we see in the passage we read?"

"Not really. In the Scripture step you generally just write down the reference to the passage. What *you're* talking about happens in the next step, Observation. However, some people write out the entire passage in their journals as the Scripture step. This is especially helpful if you're trying to memorize that passage, since writing it out in longhand will make it easier to remember. But in the interest of time, I'll just write down the reference to the passage, 'Matthew 4:1–11.'"

After she had done so, Sharon said, "Next comes Observation. I'll go ahead and write that heading in the notebook. There are at least two parts to this step. One is what you observe *in* the passage. Another is how God is speaking to you *from* the passage. And remember, this step is different from the third step of SOAP, Application, which is how to *apply* what God is speaking to you from the passage. So what do you observe in this passage?"

Victoria pondered for a bit. "What *I* observe are three temptations by the devil, and Jesus quoting the Bible to the devil each time."

"Very good!" affirmed Sharon. "Anything else?"

Victoria looked puzzled. "I'm not sure what you mean."

"Well, what condition was Jesus in when the devil tempted him, and what might we learn from that?" Sharon prompted.

"Oh, *I* see what you mean. Jesus had been fasting for forty days so he was hungry and probably tired. Is that what you're getting at, that we are more vulnerable to temptation when we are tired and hungry?"

"Exactly. Our Enemy tends to exploit our weaknesses, and one of those weaknesses could be physical. Good. What about the *kinds* of temptations that the devil threw at Jesus?"

Victoria thought for a bit and scanned the passage on her phone. "OK, the first temptation seems to have been food, or something he was craving physically. The second temptation I'm not so sure about. And the third temptation was to worship the devil, wasn't it? Meaning, idolatry?"

"Pretty good. When Josh preaches this passage, he says that the devil tempted Jesus along the three classic lines of the world, the flesh, and the devil, which means that the devil tempted Jesus in *all* the ways that it is possible to be tempted. The ordering is

slightly different in this passage; the temptation to abuse Jesus'
power by changing stones into bread was a temptation of the
flesh, because Jesus was so hungry at the time. The temptation to
throw himself down from the temple and be caught by the angels
was actually a temptation of the world, because it would demonstrate Jesus' power and invulnerability before a worldwide audience, or at least an audience at the center of the Jewish world.
And the temptation to fall down and worship the devil is, as
you've said, a temptation of the devil, which is idolatry."

Sharon glanced at her phone again. "Do you see anything unusual about the passages of Scripture that Jesus quoted? Does the
app on your phone have footnotes that give the Scripture references?"

"Yes, it does. Let me check them out." Victoria clicked on each
reference and examined the pop-up windows. "Looks like each
of them is from Deuteronomy.[28] That's in the Old Testament,
right? Is there something significant about Deuteronomy?"

Sharon shrugged. "Well, *I* think so. Deuteronomy is the last of
the five books of Moses, which are called the Law of Moses. It's
interesting that Jesus quoted the Law to the devil, that he coun-
tered the commands of the devil with the commands of God. It
makes sense because the commands of God tell us about the
character of God." Sharon remembered something else she had
observed. "Oh, did you catch the part where the devil quoted
Scripture to Jesus? What did you make of it?"

Victoria made a face. "I wondered about that. Did the devil use
Scripture correctly? I mean, what he quoted didn't really seem to
apply, did it?"

"Right!" exclaimed Sharon. "The devil was quoting Scripture
out of context trying to get Jesus to do something that the Bible
never commanded or encouraged. The verses that the devil
quoted were never meant to be used to twist God's arm into

protecting someone when they do something foolish. We need to be careful of that too, and to avoid using Scripture as a club just to get God to do what we want. We also need to realize that the devil knows Scripture better than we do and can bend it to suit his purposes."

Sharon took another look at the app on her phone. "One last thing. What might we be able to learn from the final verse, verse 11?"

Victoria studied that verse for a few moments in silence. "I'm not quite sure, unless you mean that quoting the Bible actually drove the devil away."

"Perfect! That's *exactly* what I had in mind. Jesus used Scripture as a weapon to defeat the devil's attacks. Are you familiar with the passage in Ephesians 6 that talks about putting on the whole armor of God? Here, let me find it and read it for you." Sharon searched for it on her phone and began to read.

> Put on the whole armor of God, that you may be able to stand against the schemes of the devil. For we do not wrestle against flesh and blood, but against the rulers, against the authorities, against the cosmic powers over this present darkness, against the spiritual forces of evil in the heavenly places. Therefore take up the whole armor of God, that you may be able to withstand in the evil day, and having done all, to stand firm. Stand therefore, having fastened on the belt of truth, and having put on the breastplate of righteousness, and, as shoes for your feet, having put on the readiness given by the gospel of peace. In all circumstances take up the shield of faith, with which you can extinguish all the flaming darts of the evil one; and take the helmet of salvation, and the sword of the Spirit, which is the word of God, praying at all times in the Spirit, with all

prayer and supplication. To that end, keep alert with all perseverance, making supplication for all the saints[.][29]

"The apostle Paul is encouraging us here to put on spiritual armor in order to fight the devil. Each piece of that armor—like truth, righteousness, faith, and salvation—is useful in withstanding temptation. But notice that the only offensive weapon that Paul describes is the Bible, the Word of God. That's exactly how Jesus used it in our passage in Matthew. Jesus fought back with the Bible, and the devil retreated."

Sharon grinned and said, "OK, now I really *do* have one last thing. Which of the three types of temptation—the world, the flesh, or the devil—do you think you are most susceptible to?"

Victoria grimaced a bit because the question evoked a twinge of recognition. "I was afraid that you might ask me something like that. I have a hard time with the very first kind of temptation that Jesus encountered, the temptation of the flesh. Especially in not being very nice when I'm tired or depressed or haven't had enough coffee in the morning. Let's face it—on some mornings I need coffee just to make the coffee. Most of the time this affects me at work, but it can also happen with my family too."

"Thanks for being honest, Victoria. For me it's more like the second temptation that Jesus faced, the temptation of the world, because I can struggle with pride and with what other people think about me. I guess I always want them to look up to me as the pastor's wife, sometimes for good reasons, sometimes for not-so-good reasons." She paused. "Do you want to record the observations we've just made in the notebook? Both the observations about the passage itself and the observations about how God might be using the passage to speak directly to us?"

"Sure," responded Victoria. Sharon handed her the notebook. Victoria spent a few minutes writing brief sentences under the

"Observations" heading, asking a clarification question or two along the way. When she had finished, she said, "Application is the next step, right? Should I write that heading in the notebook?"

"Please do. In fact, could you take over the notebook from here? And how do you think God is leading you to apply what we've read in this passage?"

"Well, one obvious thing is for me to memorize Scripture like you've been encouraging me to do. At least, it seems like Jesus fought back against the devil with Scripture that he had memorized. Another thing ..." Victoria thought for a moment. "I guess another thing would be to recognize when I am tired or cranky and to be especially careful during those times, or to ask God for help, so that I don't blow it and snap at somebody."

"Agreed. Me too. And I really need to watch my motivation when I'm around people at church to make sure that it is really God who is leading me to do something instead of my pride and my desire to be admired. I need to ask for God's wisdom before I volunteer to do something, or say 'Yes' to someone who wants me to do something."

"So are these the kinds of things I should be writing down under the 'Application' heading in the notebook?"

"Yes, and when you're done with that could you compose a prayer and write it under the final heading, the one for 'Prayer'? Prayer is the last step of the SOAP method. If you want, you can use the ACTS Prayer outline. Besides, you're the English major, right?" said Sharon with a wink.

"OK, just give me a minute here." Victoria finished the Application section, put down the pen, and thought for a bit. Then she wrote the "Prayer" heading and several sentences in the notebook. "How about something like this for the Prayer section? It's not really an ACTS Prayer, but instead more like a prayer for

God's help during temptation." She read aloud from the notebook. "God, please help us to be aware of when the devil is tempting us and how we should respond. Encourage us to memorize Scripture so that we can use your words in our fight against the devil. Help Victoria in particular to recognize when the devil is tempting her because she is tired or upset at work, and help Sharon to recognize when the devil is tempting her through her pride and her desire to be admired at church. We pray that your words will help us beat the devil at his own game, just like Jesus did. Amen."

"Wonderful! Let me use those exact words as our prayer as we close." Sharon bowed her head and prayed the prayer that Victoria had just written in the notebook. Then the two women talked about other things, laughed, hugged, and left for home.

Spiritual Journal

<u>Scripture:</u> Matthew 4:1-11

<u>Observation</u>
This passage describes three temptations by the devil, with Jesus quoting Scripture to the devil from Deuteronomy each time. Jesus had been fasting for forty days and was probably hungry and tired. The three temptations represented temptation of the flesh, the world, and the devil, respectively. The devil quoted Scripture too, but out of context. Jesus' resistance and quotations of the Bible drove the devil away, which brought the temptation to an end.

<u>Application</u>
Memorize Scripture to use during times of temptation. Be especially careful during times of crankiness and hunger. Ask for God's wisdom to make sure that it is really God who is leading you to do something instead of your own pride and desire to be admired.

<u>Prayer</u>
God, please help us to be aware of when the devil is tempting us and how we should respond. Encourage us to memorize Scripture so that we can use your words in our fight against the devil. Help Victoria in particular to recognize when the devil is tempting her because she is tired or upset at work, and help Sharon to recognize when the devil is tempting her through her pride and her desire to be admired at church. We pray that your words will help us beat the devil at his own game, just like Jesus did. Amen.

Sharon and Victoria's Shared Spiritual Journal

FINALIZING THE
MEMORIZATION PROCESS

The following day, Sharon tackled some chores around the house
after she got the kids off to school. As she cleaned, her thoughts
turned to her spiritual life and her desire to hide more Scripture
in her heart so that the Holy Spirit could bring it back to her mind
when she needed it. Because she was on a roll a few days ago,
Sharon wanted to continue the process of memorization that she
had begun. Her reasoning was that she should complete the ini-
tial memorization process as quickly as possible, so that she
could shift from memorization mode to maintenance mode.

When her chore list had reached a good stopping point, she
went to the computer and printed out the passage from Philippians 4 that she was memorizing, and posted it on the family refrigerator. That way she'd be reminded of it several times a day. She
smiled because she remembered one of Josh's favorite sayings
that he'd sneak into sermons from time to time: "The family refrigerator is the modern-day altar." What Josh meant was that pa-
pers and photographs stuck on the refrigerator can play the same
role for a modern family that a stone altar did for families in the

Old Testament, as reminders of what God had done in their lives. Just as a stone altar was built in Joshua chapter 4 to remind the nation of Israel that God had stopped the flow of the Jordan river to bring them into the Promised Land,[30] so photographs and verses could be tacked onto a refrigerator to remind a family of times when God had clearly—even dramatically—intervened in their lives as well.

She started off by rehearsing the first half of the passage that she had memorized. Closing her eyes, she tried to remember the observations and memory aids that she had made, then recited verses 4 through 7 from Philippians chapter 4. Opening her eyes, she checked the text. Not bad; a few words were different here and there. "Let's try to memorize it perfectly," she said to herself. Several cycles of recitation from memory and checking the text were required for her to say it word for word. "OK, that's good enough for now," she thought. Time to move on to the second half of the passage.

Verse 8 consisted of a list of attributes to focus our minds on instead of being anxious. It began with the word "finally" as if to say, "you've prayed, you've requested, you've had your anxiety replaced by peace, now fill your mind with these things instead." There was that word "brothers" again; she vowed to memorize it as "brothers and sisters." So how to commit the list to memory? Brute force? Maybe as an acronym? THJPLCEW, for "true, honorable, just, pure, lovely, commendable, excellent (well, 'excellence'), worthy (of praise)"? Hmm. "The Honorable Josh, Pastor, Lovely, Commendable, Excellent, Worthy"? OK, that one was a stretch, a mix of acronym words and actual words, but it served the purpose. Verse 9 offered a nice contrast between the words "me" and "you," and encouraged the Philippians to model themselves after Paul so that the "God of peace" (there was that "peace" word again from verse 7) would be with them.

Phrase by phrase, chunk by chunk, she committed verses 8 and 9 to memory just as she had done for verses 4 through 7. When she felt relatively solid, she closed her eyes and reeled them off as fast as she could, checking herself against the text when she was done. A couple of words were wrong; try again. Lather, rinse, repeat. She iterated through the recite-and-check cycle several more times until she could say it perfectly.

Now to put both halves together, verses 4 through 7 with verses 8 and 9. Same deal: recite and check, recite and check. More quickly than she had anticipated, she was able to rattle off the entire passage word for word. "Thank you, Lord," she sighed in prayer. Sharon knew that when she tried it again tomorrow, a few words would be out of place and require rearranging. But tomorrow was another day.

A Quiet Time in Crisis

That evening Sharon got a call from Victoria, which was unusual because she generally texted. Even more unusually, Victoria was crying when Sharon accepted the call. "Sharon," Victoria sobbed, "my mom has breast cancer. The biopsy came back positive."

"Oh, no," exclaimed Sharon. "I'm so sorry to hear that. What are they going to do now? And can Josh and I help in any way?"

Victoria tried to compose herself. "She'll be meeting with a cancer doctor next week to figure out what to do. Maybe take the lump out. Maybe start chemotherapy. They're not sure yet."

Sharon's mind was already racing ahead. "Josh can put your mom on the church prayer list, both on the Web site and on the email list. And unfortunately, it's too late tonight and I have the women's group tomorrow night, but are you free to come over two nights from now?"

Victoria thought she might be able to do that, so Sharon set a time and closed the call with prayer. "Oh, a great psalm to cling to, both for you and for your mom, is Psalm 91," she said after she finished praying. Victoria promised to read that psalm, and ended the call.

Victoria sat in silence for several minutes. Too many thoughts and emotions jostled and jabbed for supremacy in the tournament of her mind. Finally, she sighed and stood up. She wasn't sure if she'd ever read Psalm 91, so she grabbed her Bible to find out.

Opening her Bible right in the middle, it didn't take long for Victoria to find Psalm 91. She read eagerly, because the words seemed intended just for her.

> He who dwells in the shelter of the Most High
>   will abide in the shadow of the Almighty.
> I will say to the LORD, "My refuge and my fortress,
>   my God, in whom I trust."
> For he will deliver you from the snare of the fowler
>   and from the deadly pestilence.
> He will cover you with his pinions,
>   and under his wings you will find refuge;
>   his faithfulness is a shield and buckler.
> You will not fear the terror of the night,
>   nor the arrow that flies by day,
> nor the pestilence that stalks in darkness,
>   nor the destruction that wastes at noonday.
> A thousand may fall at your side,
>   ten thousand at your right hand,
>   but it will not come near you.
> You will only look with your eyes
>   and see the recompense of the wicked.[31]

Her heart stirred within her, because she wanted God not only to be *her* refuge and strength but especially her *mom's* refuge and strength during this time of worry and uncertainty. She loved the poetic imagery of the psalm: Shadow. Shelter. Refuge. Fortress.

There were bird images: Fowler. Pinions. Wings. There were images of military protection: Shield. Buckler. She flipped open her NIV, a recent gift from Sharon, to see what a "buckler" might be. The NIV used the word "rampart," which she didn't think was quite the same thing. She'd have to come back to that. In any event, verses 5 through 8 were pretty clear: the psalm promised that God would take away any fear of military defeat or of the ravages of disease. This last part was *absolutely* her prayer for her mom.

She read ahead and discovered the basis of those promises: they (the nation of Israel, she assumed) had made God their refuge and dwelling place. As the psalm continued, the promises were elaborated, and then at the end a different person seemed to be speaking.

> Because you have made the LORD your dwelling place—
>   the Most High, who is my refuge—
> no evil shall be allowed to befall you,
>   no plague come near your tent.
> For he will command his angels concerning you
>   to guard you in all your ways.
> On their hands they will bear you up,
>   lest you strike your foot against a stone.
> You will tread on the lion and the adder;
>   the young lion and the serpent you will trample underfoot.
> "Because he holds fast to me in love, I will deliver him;
>   I will protect him, because he knows my name.
> When he calls to me, I will answer him;
>   I will be with him in trouble;
>   I will rescue him and honor him.
> With long life I will satisfy him
>   And show him my salvation."[32]

The change of speaker at the end was evidently a switch to God himself. God promised to rescue and protect those who reach out to him, perhaps even with the help of the angels mentioned right before God started to speak. In addition, God promised to grant long life and salvation to those who call on him. Transcending the myriad of images and references, the thrust of the entire psalm was consistent and clear: if someone took refuge in God, God promised to protect them.

Victoria burst into tears again, this time out of gratitude and joy. "Dear God," she prayed through her tears, "thank you for this wonderful psalm that you provided through Sharon exactly when I needed it, which spoke right to me. Help me to truly take refuge in you so that I can claim your promise of protection, and especially help my mom to take refuge in you and to trust you to protect her health. Oh God, please heal my mom and give her peace, and especially help her to believe in Jesus as her Savior and Lord. And thank you for Sharon and her friendship, and give her the energy she needs for all the things that a pastor's wife and a mother is expected to do. I pray this in the name of Jesus. Amen." She dried her eyes and got ready for bed.

Praying without Ceasing
and the Jesus Prayer

"Sometimes I just don't know how to pray, or what to pray for, or even if I want to pray at all. It's been happening more often since my mom was diagnosed with cancer. Is that normal?"

Victoria's words struck a chord deep inside Sharon's soul. Memories flooded her mind of experiencing the same thing during times of crisis or emptiness in her own life: the long dry patch in her marriage; sustained opposition at church; discipline problems at school for her oldest boy. Each of those situations had affected her prayer life, at times even bringing it to a halt. "Lord, please give me the wisdom to help Victoria with something that I don't think I've completely figured out myself," she prayed silently.

Sharon looked around the coffee shop. It was unusually busy that evening, and the only table they could find was a small one near the entrance. That table was less private than the one in the corner that they usually used. She kept her voice low as a result. "I know exactly what you mean, Victoria," Sharon reassured her. "The same thing has happened to me, and yes, I think that it is normal, especially when you're in the middle of a crisis."

"But what do I *do*?" implored Victoria, unable to suppress the emotion in her voice.

"One of the thoughts that comforts me in that situation is that prayer is an activity that God has rigged in our favor. Let me tell you what I mean," Sharon said hurriedly in response to the expression of surprise on Victoria's face. "Every member of the Godhead, the Trinity, is involved in prayer. They help us when we pray and even when we don't know *how* to pray. The Bible says that the Holy Spirit, who is the person of God who lives inside us when we come to know Jesus as our Savior,[33] intercedes on our behalf with groans too deep for words when we don't know how to pray. One way to look at this is that the Spirit takes our inability to pray and translates it into prayer that corresponds to God's will. Here's the passage of Scripture I'm referring to, in Romans chapter 8." She began to read from the Bible app on her phone.

> Likewise the Spirit helps us in our weakness. For we do not know what to pray for as we ought, but the Spirit himself intercedes for us with groanings too deep for words. And he who searches hearts knows what is the mind of the Spirit, because the Spirit intercedes for the saints according to the will of God.[34]

"And God the Son, Jesus Christ, who even now is sitting at God's right hand in bodily form in the throne room of heaven,[35] intercedes for us with God the Father too. The apostle Paul tells us about this just a few verses later in Romans 8." She scrolled down in her Bible app. "Here it is, verse 34: 'Who is to condemn? Christ Jesus is the one who died—more than that, who was raised—who is at the right hand of God, who is indeed interceding for us.'[36] The book of Hebrews tells us more about this ministry of intercession and describes Jesus as our great High Priest on the throne of grace in heaven."[37]

"Wait," interjected Victoria. "You mean *both* Jesus and the Holy Spirit are interceding for us? They're doing the same thing?"

"No, they're not really doing the same thing; they're interceding for us in different ways. The verses I just read say that the Holy Spirit intercedes for us by changing the *content* of our prayer in some way to better correspond to the will of God. By contrast, the way that Jesus intercedes for us is to press our *case* with God the Father once that prayer has been relayed by the Holy Spirit, by agreeing with our prayer and encouraging God the Father to answer it. The actual mechanics of all this are a bit of a mystery, at least to me. But the Bible is pretty clear that both the Holy Spirit and Jesus intercede for us when we pray. Does this make sense?"

Victoria nodded slowly. "I think so."

Sharon decided to stress the practical implications. "The bottom line is this. Even when I'm not sure how to pray—or just *can't* pray, for whatever reason—God has it covered. Why? Each member of the Trinity is involved in the act of prayer, whether in helping us to pray when we don't know how (that's God the Holy Spirit); in interceding for us in prayer with God the Father (that's God the Son); or in answering prayer itself (that's God the Father). I find that *really* comforting, actually."

"That *is* comforting. But is there something I can actually *do* in those situations? I mean, I know God has it covered and all. But what do I *do* when that happens, like in the situation I'm going through right now?"

"You mean, other than to relax and let God be God?" Sharon replied with a twinkle in her eyes. "I'm just teasing a bit; I know what you mean, and have wondered the same thing myself. It *is* important to rest in the security that God is in control. But I *do* think that there are things we can do when we find ourselves in that situation. One of the things that I've found helpful when I either don't *want* to pray or don't know *how* to pray is to pray Scripture back to God, to take God's own words and pray them back to him. For example, you could take one of the Psalms and pray the words or the truths behind the words back to God in the first person as if they were your own words."

"Psalm 23 would probably be a great psalm for that, right?" Victoria interjected.

"Right!" responded Sharon. "Psalm 23 is one of *my* favorites too, but there are a lot of great psalms that you could use. Another option is to find the prayers that the apostle Paul includes in almost every one of his letters and either pray them for yourself or for someone else. Let me see if I can find an example." Sharon tapped on her phone a few times. "OK, here's one, in the first chapter of Ephesians." She positioned the screen of her phone so they both could see it, and scrolled as she read.

> For this reason, because I have heard of your faith in the Lord Jesus and your love toward all the saints, I do not cease to give thanks for you, remembering you in my prayers, that the God of our Lord Jesus Christ, the Father of glory, may give you the Spirit of wisdom and of revelation in the knowledge of him, having the eyes of your hearts enlightened, that you may know what is the hope to which he has called you, what are the riches of his glorious inheritance in the saints, and what is the immeasurable greatness of his power toward us who believe, according to the working of his great might that he worked in Christ when he raised him from the dead and seated him at his right hand in the heavenly places, far above all rule and authority and power and dominion, and above every name that is

named, not only in this age but also in the one to come. And he put all things under his feet and gave him as head over all things to the church, which is his body, the fullness of him who fills all in all.[38]

Sharon looked up at Victoria. "You see how powerful that could be, to take a prayer intended for a particular situation and to apply it in general? And to make it your own by praying it back to God, either for yourself or for someone else? I mean, who *wouldn't* want God to give them a Spirit of wisdom and revelation in the knowledge of God, or to have their hearts enlightened so that they could truly know the hope that God has called them to and the rich inheritance he has given them in Glory? Or to know the greatness of God's power in raising Jesus from the dead and seating him at his right hand in the heavenly throne room?"

"Wow, I never thought of it like that before. That's pretty cool. I'd love to have somebody pray a prayer like that for me."

Sharon stopped for a moment and transitioned to a new topic. "But there's another example of praying Scripture back to God that I've found especially helpful, especially in times of severe emotional crisis when I had no idea how to pray, or even whether I wanted to pray at all. Situations that sound a lot like what you are going through with your mom. Have you heard of the Jesus Prayer?"

Victoria shook her head. "No, I haven't. Is that one of Jesus' own prayers in the Bible?"

"Actually, it's a short prayer *to* Jesus based on a parable of Jesus and the plea for healing that a blind man made to Jesus," clarified Sharon. "It has become very popular and widely used by Christians in many parts of the world. The parable is found in Luke chapter 18,[39] which contrasts the arrogant way a Pharisee prayed with the humble way a tax collector prayed. The plea of the blind man is found later on in the same chapter.[40] But the form in which the Jesus Prayer is usually prayed is this: 'Lord Jesus Christ, Son of God, have mercy on me, a sinner.' Short. Sweet. Simple. But there's a lot in that prayer if you look hard at it."

Victoria frowned. "I'm not sure I get the point. Why is this prayer so popular? And when should I pray it, exactly?"

Sharon debated with herself about the best way to proceed. "Let me try to answer your questions from two perspectives. One perspective is the power and compactness of the prayer itself. Inside that short prayer is the truth about our need, the truth about God's mercy, and a plea for God's mercy to meet our need. It's the gospel in a nutshell. At least for me, the times when I need God's mercy the most are when I'm so emotionally distraught that I have no idea how to pray. About all I can bring myself to do is to pray for God's mercy. Clarity about *how* to pray only comes later, after the emotion has passed. The Jesus Prayer lets me throw myself at Jesus' feet and beg for mercy and grace in the midst of my crisis. And the great thing is that Jesus loves to say 'Yes!' to the Jesus Prayer, to an acknowledgement of who *he* really is and who *we* really are and a request for mercy on that basis. You can see that 'Yes!' in Luke 18 as well."[41]

"What do you mean?" asked Victoria with a puzzled expression on her face.

"I mean that Jesus answered 'Yes!' both times the Jesus Prayer was prayed in Luke 18. He declared that the tax collector was justified before God, but not the Pharisee. And he healed the blind man by restoring his sight. Humbly asking for mercy is a powerful way to pray."

Sharon took a sip of her chai, to which she had treated herself because she had accumulated enough points for a free drink. "There's another use for the Jesus Prayer, which can be considered a 'steady state' use instead of a 'crisis event' use. Are you familiar with that great set of verses in 1 Thessalonians chapter 5? I memorized them once; let me see if I can recall them for you." She waited for the memory neurons to fire. "Rejoice always, pray without ceasing, give thanks in all circumstances; for this is the will of God in Christ Jesus for you."[42]

Grateful that the Holy Spirit had brought back to her mind the Word of God that she had hidden in her heart, Sharon pressed on. "Let's take a look at these short verses. Three commands: rejoice, pray, give thanks. And significantly, the apostle Paul claims that obeying these commands is the will of God. You know how much time each of us spends praying that God would reveal his will? Well, here's a shining example of the will of God spelled out about as plainly as you can get. But the question is, *how* do we obey this expressed will of God? In particular, how do we obey the command to 'pray without ceasing'[43]? The Church through the ages has developed several practices in response to this command, and one has been to pray the Jesus Prayer throughout the day to keep the prayer connection alive. Prayer is performed continually by persisting in the state of prayer. In other words, viewing prayer as a *state* instead of an *event*, as something you *are* instead of just something you *do*, is a way that the Church can obey the command to pray continually. Though it didn't explicitly use the Jesus Prayer, that was the whole point of a famous book called *The Practice of the Presence of God*. It was written by a monk who worked in a monastery as a cook; I think his name was Brother Lawrence. Does this make sense so far?"

Victoria slowly nodded. "I think so. Maybe. Can you give me an example?"

"Sure. One thing you can do with the Jesus Prayer to pray it continually is to link it with a bodily process that humans do all the time. Namely, with breathing. You can divide the Jesus Prayer into two halves. The first half is, 'Lord Jesus Christ, Son of God.'

The second half is, 'have mercy on me, a sinner.' Now link the first half with breathing in, and the second half with breathing out. That choice was not arbitrary; if you think of breathing in as receiving positive things that benefit you (like oxygen), then what you are receiving in the first half of the Jesus Prayer is that Jesus is the Christ—in other words, the promised Messiah, the Anointed One—who is the Son of God. And if you think of breathing out as expelling negative things that are bad for you (like carbon dioxide), then what you are expelling in the second half of the Jesus Prayer is your condition as a sinner that makes you implore God for mercy. Of course, Christians are *redeemed* sinners, not *hopeless* sinners. But since we *remain* sinners, we will always need God's mercy."

"Hmm," mused Victoria, who was trying that suggestion on for size.

Sharon tried to be more specific. "Let me get really, really practical here. In times of crisis, or anytime you don't know either how to pray or even if you *want* to pray—like what you've been going through since your mom was diagnosed with cancer—you can pray the Jesus Prayer because it is universally true, true for all Christians at all times and in all places. Affirm the deity and power of Christ. Ask for his mercy to comfort you and to transform you and your situation to the point that you are better able to pray. Then trust that the Trinity, each of the members of the Godhead, will follow through on their promises in Scripture and intercede for you with the Father who hears and answers your prayers. And in more calm, steady-state times, you could obey the command to pray continually by linking the Jesus Prayer to your breathing and keep the prayer connection with God alive throughout the day."

She was reminded of an important point and hurriedly added, "But there's a crucial thing to keep in mind. Prayer is not a magic incantation that we use to bend God to *our* will. Instead, it is a conversation in which we bend our lives to *his* will. Meaning, the Jesus Prayer is not a mantra that we repeat until we get what we want. Like any other prayer, our motivation for praying the Jesus Prayer should be conversation, relationship, and obedience."

Victoria nodded her head. "That makes sense. Let me think about what you've told me, and I'll try out the Jesus Prayer sometime. It might be helpful right about now."

The two women moved on to discuss other areas of their lives, such as the latest news from church and the treatment options for Victoria's mom, and exchanged prayer requests as the coffee shop became increasingly less busy. They lost track of time, only regaining it when the baristas began their not-so-subtle process of turning off the lights to the sections of the shop one-by-one.

13

Teaching *Lectio Divina*

One Saturday morning Sharon invited Victoria over to her house so they could have a bit more privacy than was possible in the coffee shop. Sharon and her family lived in a modest split-level house in one of the older neighborhoods that radiated off of Downtown. The reason for the privacy was that Sharon wanted to introduce Victoria to the practice of *Lectio Divina*.

Victoria brought freshly baked brownies because she couldn't shake the voice of her mother in her head, who always stressed, "Never show up empty-handed, *mi hija*." She unwrapped the plate as Sharon poured out coffee and tea. "Thanks for coming over this morning," Sharon said. "The boys are out with their dad for a couple of hours, so we'll have some time to ourselves."

"Can you tell me again what you wanted to talk with me about?" Victoria asked.

"Sure. I wanted to tell you about another way to meet God in the Bible. We talked at first about how to have a Quiet Time, and then about Spiritual Journaling, which is just a way of structuring a Quiet Time by using a notebook and the SOAP method. What I want to introduce to you this morning is something called *Lectio*

Divina" (Sharon pronounced it "**lek**-tee-oh di-**vee**-na"[44]), "which just means 'sacred reading' in Latin. It's a practice with a long history in the Church, but these days it's more well-known in some parts of the Church than in others. Josh first learned about it in seminary, but not in any course that he took. A fellow student who became his prayer partner taught it to him."

"Huh," said Victoria. "What do you *do* in *Lectio Divina*?"

"Well, you read the Bible," Sharon joked. "OK, not quite; there's more to it than that. Actually, the way *Lectio Divina* is usually taught is as a four-step procedure. Each step has a Latin name too, but I'll just give you an English word to remember it by, generally one beginning with the letter 'r.' You can use that name as a mnemonic device—a memory aid—so that you can remember what to do in that step. Ready?"

Victoria nodded. She was thinking, "This sounds kinda different," but kept her thoughts to herself.

Sharon plunged in. "The first step is Read. Obviously, in this step you read the Bible. But you do more than that; you read the passage in the Bible several times slowly, out loud if you can, and really try to observe what's being said. Don't be satisfied with a surface understanding of the passage. Instead, dig in deep and try to make connections, both inside the passage itself and between that passage and other passages in the Bible. You can think of this step as doing a mini Bible study which forms the basis for all of the other steps.

She took a chewy bite of brownie. "The second step is Reflect. In this step you meditate on what you just read. A good Bible verse that describes this step is Psalm 1, verse 2, which says, 'his delight is in the law of the Lord, and on his law he meditates day and night.'[45] You can see from this verse that meditation is intentional and focused and takes time; nevertheless, meditation is a delight, not a chore. Meditation is generally not random; the best way to do it is to structure it in some way. What *I* like to do is to *visualize*, to create pictures in my mind based on reflection on the passage. You can organize the visualization along *time* lines, like projecting yourself back in time and picturing yourself in the middle of the situation described by the passage. Then you can move forward in time and project the world of the passage into your own world in the present day. Or you can organize it along *space* lines and mentally explore the geographical location in which the passage is set, or other geographical locations that come to mind including your own location. Or you can even organize it along *personal* lines and meditate on situations and people that the passage reminds you of, and the ways in which those memories are similar to or different from the passage. This step can be *very* imaginative and can really make the passage come alive in your mind."

Victoria pursed her lips in puzzlement. "Is this what you mean by meditation, to create pictures in your mind from the passage in order to understand it better? If so, it sounds kind of like something we learned in poetry class in college."

Sharon nodded in agreement. "Yes, that does sound similar. And it took me some time and practice to get comfortable with it. But ever since, visualizing the Bible as part of the meditation process has been like reading the Bible in color instead of black and white. We'll get a chance to practice it together in a few minutes."

She collected her thoughts and pressed on. "OK, that's the first two steps. The third step is Respond. In this step you pray God's Word back to him, in his own words, often from many of the perspectives that you identified during the meditation step. This is where *you* communicate with *God* on the basis of his Word."

Her tea was getting cold, so Sharon walked over to the microwave to heat it up. "The last step is Rest. In this step you rest in

God's presence and let *him* speak to *you* like *you* spoke to *him* in the previous step. By resting you are creating a silent space in which you listen and receive what God has to tell you through his Word. The goal is not to empty your mind into insignificant nothingness; instead, the purpose is to clear your mind of noise and chatter so that it can be filled with the significant something of the voice of God in the passage. This mental silence allows you to focus on how God is present with you and is speaking to you personally."

She interrupted her explanation to help herself to another brownie. "These are really good; thanks for bringing them."

Victoria made a face. "Thanks; it's one of the few family recipes I actually know how to make. I think I was motivated to learn because it goes so well with coffee."

Sharon finished the brownie and licked her fingers. "A couple of good Bible verses describe what is happening in this step. One of them is from Psalm 46: 'Be still, and know that I am God.'[46] Another is from 1 Samuel, when Samuel was a boy and heard the voice of God one night. He responded to God with, 'Speak, for your servant hears.'[47] So this is the step in which you really meet God in the Bible, and *God* communicates with *you* on the basis of his Word."

Since Victoria seemed to be following her, Sharon wrapped up her overview. "This four-step process is the traditional way that *Lectio Divina* is taught. But some people add two additional steps, a preparation step at the beginning called Prepare and an action or application step at the end called Act. When we practice this together in a few minutes I'll probably include these steps as well. And just like we talked about when we discussed Spiritual Journaling, you can journal the whole process if you want. This might be a great thing to do, at least for the first few times you try *Lectio*

Divina, in order to help you learn it. You can think of it as an optional step called Record."

14

PRACTICING *LECTIO DIVINA*: PREPARE AND READ

Sharon looked at Victoria quizzically. "Do you have any questions or areas of confusion I can help with before we try this out?"

Victoria shook her head. "I mean, I'm not really sure about it, but I'm hoping that things will become clearer when we do it together."

Sharon nodded. "Good. I agree. But first let's prepare our hearts for meeting God in his Word, which is the Prepare step I just mentioned. What I generally like to do in this step is to read aloud a Bible verse that talks about preparation. Some of my favorites are a couple I've told you about before, from Psalm 19 and Psalm 51.[48] There's a good one in Psalm 119, too: 'Open my eyes, that I may behold wondrous things out of your law.'[49] Another choice is the Jesus Prayer. Yet another could be a very Trinitarian prayer based on 1 Corinthians chapter 2: 'Heavenly Father, by the power of your Holy Spirit who inspired your Word, please reveal to me the mind of Christ.'[50] There are lots of other verses you could use directly or model a prayer after. In our case, let's go ahead and use the one from Psalm 19. Could you read that aloud for us as an opening prayer? It's Psalm 19, verse 14."

Victoria found it in her Bible and read it out loud. She looked up at Sharon expectantly. "The Read step is next, right?"

"Right. Let's use a familiar passage for the Read step for learning purposes, at least a familiar one for me. The one I'm thinking of is that great passage in the last chapter of Philippians that I've mentioned to you before. I've been memorizing it lately. I'll try to recite it for you to start things off." She closed her eyes and retrieved it from memory.

> Rejoice in the Lord always; again I will say, rejoice. Let your reasonableness be known to everyone. The Lord is at hand; do not be anxious about anything, but in everything by prayer and supplication with thanksgiving let your requests be made known to God. And the peace of God, which surpasses all understanding, will guard your hearts and your minds in Christ Jesus.
>
> Finally, brothers, whatever is true, whatever is honorable, whatever is just, whatever is pure, whatever is lovely, whatever is commendable, if there is any excellence, if there is anything worthy of praise, think about these things. What you have learned and received and heard and seen in me—practice these things, and the God of peace will be with you.[51]

Sharon made a mental note of a few words that she had trouble retrieving. "Except for the fact that I said it from memory, what I just did was the first part of the Read step, which is to read the passage through slowly and out loud. Right off the top of your head, what are some things that you noticed about the passage? Did you pick up any themes or repeated words or phrases?"

Victoria thought for a moment. "Rejoice. Pray. Peace. Don't worry. That kind of thing?"

Sharon nodded. "Exactly. Great start. But we don't want to stop there. We want to read the passage *several* times, slowly and carefully, and observe everything we can, all of the details and all of the connections. How about you read it back to me?" Victoria turned to the passage in her Bible and read it aloud. "Thanks," Sharon said. "Let's take a couple of minutes and read it silently to ourselves a few times." When they were finished Sharon asked, "Did you notice anything more?"

"Not really," said Victoria. "Except that the person who wrote this—it was Paul, right? —seems to be saying, 'Don't do this; instead do that.' I mean, he starts off by saying 'Rejoice!' Then he says, 'Don't worry; instead, pray and you will receive peace.' Or, 'pray, ask, and give thanks, and you will receive peace.' Then he says, 'Think about positive things instead of negative things.' Well, he didn't actually say 'instead of negative things,' but he seems to have implied it. Then he ends with 'follow my example and you will also receive peace,' which I think was his example of praying instead of worrying, and of focusing on the positive instead of on the negative."

"Very good! I don't know what you were thinking when you said, 'Not really.' You picked up on a lot of things in that passage."

"Thanks! What did *you* observe?"

"A lot of the same things that you did, actually. But I've studied Philippians before, and Josh has preached a couple of sermon series on Philippians over the years. You know how the passage starts off with the command to rejoice? Well, joy in general and rejoicing in particular is a major theme in Philippians, probably the most important theme. For example, the same command to 'rejoice in the Lord' was made in the previous chapter, word for word.[52] And what's striking about that theme is that Paul is not writing this from the comfort of his own home. Instead, he is writing this in prison, probably with a guard standing outside of his cell. I think that influenced his choice of language; notice that he said that the peace that comes through prayer would 'guard your hearts and your minds in Christ Jesus.'"[53]

Sharon went on. "It's pretty clear that Paul had learned these lessons the hard way. He learned to rejoice and pray and focus on the positive as a result of all that he had suffered because he wouldn't stop preaching the gospel. What he seems to be telling the Philippians is that they shouldn't find their joy and their peace in their circumstances, but instead in the Lord Jesus and all that he has done for them. Just a few verses later he will say that he had learned to be content in every situation in which he had found himself, whether a situation of comfort or a situation of hardship.[54] 'I can do all things through him who strengthens me'[55] is the most important lesson that God had taught him."

"Wow, that's a really good lesson to learn. But it's an easy lesson to forget when your life is crashing down around your ears."

"It sure is. That's why we need the constant reminder of the truth in this passage, not just that we should take our circumstances and give them to the Lord and claim his peace, but especially that we need to rely on *Christ's* strength to do that instead of our *own* strength."

Practicing *Lectio Divina*:
Reflect

Sharon assessed their progress. "I think we've done a good job on the Read step. We've read the passage several times and observed a lot of important things, not just things on the surface but things that are deeper. Let's move on to Reflect. This is where *Lectio Divina* gets, well, *interesting*, especially if you've never done it before. Maybe we can approach this step as an exercise in guided visualization, where we use the passage to create images in our minds from several perspectives. First let me tell you where I might be going in this step. I think I might start out back in the time of Paul and look at the passage from his perspective, and then from the perspective of the church in Philippi. Then I'll probably move forward in time and look at the passage from other perspectives. There are a lot of choices here, a lot of perspectives we could adopt, but we'll start there. OK?"

"OK," Victoria replied somewhat uncertainly. "Maybe I can get the hang of it by following your example."

Sharon closed her eyes so that she could start the visualization process without distractions. "Picture the apostle Paul sitting in jail writing a letter to the church in Philippi. A guard stands right outside his cell. Paul had endured a lot of pain and hardship during his imprisonment. Yet God had used those trials to teach Paul not to find his happiness and identity in his circumstances, but instead to find it in his relationship with Christ and in all that Christ had suffered on his behalf. That's why the letter to the Philippians is so counterintuitive, so full of joy instead of bitterness, because Paul had learned through trials how to be content in whatever circumstances God chose to bring into his life. And now he is telling the Philippian church how they can do the same thing in the midst of their own trials."

Having constructed the picture frame, Sharon painted in the details. "So Paul begins our passage by stating a general principle, but as a command: 'Rejoice in the Lord always.' And he repeats it for emphasis: 'Again I will say, rejoice.'[56] He passes on to the Philippian church the same lesson he has had to learn himself, that their lives should be characterized by gentleness and reasonableness, not worry and complaint. And then he tells them *how* to do so by identifying a procedure for mental health and ministry effectiveness. Paul had to learn this procedure the hard way because of opposition and imprisonment. What he had learned was to implore God in prayer to meet all of his needs, but with thanksgiving because he trusted that God was good and would answer his prayer. After prayer comes the promise of peace that is beyond understanding, because there is no logical reason for that peace in the midst of those circumstances other than the promise of God. Just as the soldier outside the cell is guarding Paul in the power of the Roman Empire, so the peace that God promises through prayer will guard our hearts and minds in the power of Christ Jesus. Picture the apostle Paul practicing that procedure over and over in his cell as he petitioned God in prayer for a whole host of concerns, like the safety of his brothers and sisters in Israel, or the health and vitality of the churches he had founded, or especially his own future and the possibility of his impending death."

Sharon opened her eyes and looked over at Victoria. "Are you with me so far?"

Victoria nodded. "I think so. You're not done with the passage, right?"

"No, not with the passage *or* the perspectives. But do you see what is going on in the Reflect step? The goal is to take what you've learned in the Read step and visually explore the nooks and crannies of the world of the passage in your mind from multiple perspectives and timeframes, whether then or now or throughout history. It is this kind of meditation that can really make the passage come alive and pop for you, so that you can see *yourself* inside the text. First let me finish the passage, and then we can try to picture other perspectives."

Sharon picked up where she left off. "Now that Paul has told the Philippian church what they *shouldn't* focus on, namely their own circumstances which have been laid at Jesus' feet in prayer, he turns to what they *should* focus on. Things that are true, honorable, just, pure, lovely, commendable, excellent, praiseworthy—*these* are the things that should fill their minds. And notice the order here. Focusing on the good things is only possible *after* you have given the difficult things over to God in prayer and asked for his strength to think about good things instead. Finally, Paul holds himself up as a model for the Philippian church, and in effect says, 'Just as God has taught *me* these lessons, I can help teach *you* these lessons by the way I have learned to live my life. And God will bless you with peace as you follow my example.' Form an image in your mind of Paul practicing these lessons himself through a continuous cycle of prayer, release, and refocus. Picture him laying his fear for his life at Jesus' feet and focusing

instead on Jesus' love for him and his calling as an apostle to the
Gentiles. Picture him claiming God's promise of peace both in
and despite his circumstances. And picture him recognizing the
higher calling behind those circumstances, that not only was God
forming *him* for effective ministry and growth in grace, but God
was also using those circumstances as a ministry to *others* who
were facing difficult circumstances of their own."

Sharon sat up straight in her chair and rolled out a kink in her
neck. "OK, that's visualization from Paul's perspective. And I tend
to start with the perspective of the original writer or main character when I do the Reflect step. But there's a lot of freedom here,
and many possible options. Do you want to pick up the visualization from another perspective yourself?"

Victoria frowned and pondered the question. "I'm not sure I'm
ready yet. This is different than what I've been doing in my Quiet
Times. Could you keep going so that I can see an example of how
an entire Reflect step could be done?"

"Sure. Let me adopt three more perspectives: the perspective
of the Philippian church; my perspective; and your perspective.
Sound good?"

Victoria made an involuntary expression of surprise. "*My* perspective? What do you mean?"

"You'll see. I'll keep going, OK? Let's picture the church in Philippi and the difficult circumstances they were in. Opposition
from the community.[57] Challenges from rogue Christians who
wanted to return to the Law of Moses.[58] Leadership struggles inside the church itself.[59] And now they get this letter from Paul
that commanded them to rejoice, to pray, to give their concerns
over to God and claim his peace, and to focus on other things
than their circumstances. Visualize them hearing this for the first
time as Paul's letter was read to them during a worship service.
Picture some of the leaders being stung as Paul called them out

by name and ordered them to reconcile. Their behavior was in stark contrast to the image that Paul had painted earlier in the letter of the humility of Jesus and his sacrificial example that should have unified them already.[60] Picture others in leadership catching Paul's vision and calling the congregation to the practices of joy, prayer, petition, and peace. Visualize them praying for their hostile community, for the misguided Christians who insisted that Gentiles should follow the Law of Moses, and for their own divided leadership. Picture the peace that God had promised descending on them as they united in joy over the reconciliation and contentment that Christ's sacrifice had purchased for them."

"Wow, you must have studied Philippians pretty well to be able to do that," exclaimed Victoria.

"Well, the more you know the Bible the better you're able to visualize it," Sharon admitted. She switched gears. "Now for my own perspective. We've talked in confidence before about some of the challenges that our church is facing. When I read this passage, I hear Paul commanding me to rejoice that God is in control, instead of worrying about those who are opposing Josh's leadership or who have left the church. I picture myself taking all of my concerns about the church, giving them to Jesus in prayer, and receiving the peace that is promised regardless of the circumstances. I visualize myself focusing on positive things instead—on the wonderful family that God has given me; on the progress that the church has made over the long term; and especially on all the riches that I have in Christ. And I picture myself serving as a model of contentment and peace for others in the congregation, including you, so that I can pass on the lessons I have learned from God just like Paul did."

Sharon raised her eyebrows and looked at Victoria. "Unless you're ready to jump in, I'd like to try to picture things from your perspective." Victoria nodded her head slowly. "So ... I see you hearing Paul's words and immediately thinking about the situation with your mom. I picture you being really challenged about how to find joy in that situation and break the cycle of worry and sleeplessness. But I also picture you taking your love for your mom and your worry about your mom's health and giving them to God in prayer. This may need to be something you do *frequently*, over a long period of time, until it becomes a habit. But I can see you being blessed by the peace that God promises, and learning how to rest in and find joy in that peace. I picture you focusing instead on other wonderful gifts that God has given you—your new life in Christ and all the positive changes that have come with it; your new church home filled with people who love and accept you; and your friendship with me, which I am blessed by and grateful for. And I see you serving as a witness to your colleagues at work because of the joy they see in you in the midst of a difficult, emotional situation."

"*Now* I see what you meant about my own perspective," responded Victoria. "Thanks for that; it was a great way to see myself in the passage."

PRACTICING *LECTIO DIVINA*: RESPOND, REST, ACT

Sharon refreshed their drinks before moving on. "Respond comes next; this is the prayer step where you pray the passage back to God. We've talked about things like this before, like praying a psalm back to God in the first person. But in *Lectio Divina*, the prayer step builds on the insights learned in the Read and Reflect steps. And you'll probably want to pray with the passage right in front of you, so this could be an example of prayer with eyes wide open. Let me start us off, and if you feel comfortable, maybe you could chime in, OK?"

"OK," replied Victoria. "This step seems more like things that we've done before."

Sharon turned back a page to the first verse of the passage in Philippians 4 and began to pray. "Heavenly Father, we rejoice in who you are and what you have done, and we ask for your strength to rejoice in you at all times. Please work in our hearts so that we are always gentle and reasonable to others, and may we always live as if you are near to us instead of far away. We praise you for the peace that you promise when we put aside our anxiety and instead lay our burdens and requests at your feet, with thanksgiving because we know that you are faithful to your promises. Just as there was a soldier who guarded the apostle Paul in his cell, we claim your promise that your peace will guard our hearts and minds in your Son Jesus Christ. And we know that this peace is beyond understanding because it could only have come from you, not our circumstances."

She raised her head to look at Victoria. "Do you want to try to take it from here? Did you get the hang of what I was doing in this step?"

Victoria nodded hesitantly. "You were just rewording the passage a bit so that you could pray it back to God as if it came from you, right?"

"Exactly," Sharon responded.

"Well, OK. I'll give it a try." Victoria turned the page in her Bible to the next verse. She took a moment to compose her thoughts. "God, after we have taken all of our worries and given them to you in prayer, give us the strength to focus on positive things instead of the things that are worrying us. Give us the insight to recognize all of the *true* things around us, the honorable things, the just and pure and lovely things, the things that are commendable and excellent and worthy of praise. Help us to think about these things instead of all of our problems. And help us to be good examples to others of how to give you our problems in prayer and focus on positive things instead, so that they can receive your peace too. I thank you for the good model that Sharon has been to me in doing these things, especially in helping me cope with my mom's cancer."

Victoria stopped because she had choked up. Sharon reached out and squeezed her arm to comfort her. "I know how hard this is for you. While we're still in the prayer step, can I pray for both of us that we give our problems to God and receive his peace? I know that this borrows a bit from the next steps of *Lectio Divina*, but it seems like the right thing to do."

Victoria nodded and wiped the tears from her cheeks. "Go ahead. Thanks."

Sharon closed her eyes. "Father God, you know all of our problems and our prayer requests even before we pray them. We ask that Victoria would be able to give you her worry and fear about her mom's health, and live in peace instead of in constant anxiety. We pray that in your grace and mercy you would do the same thing for her mom, and would heal her of the cancer they have found in her body. And we pray that I would be able to give my worry about the political situation at church over to you too, and that you would heal the division that seems to have gotten worse in the last few months. Help us to focus on the truth that you are our sovereign God who is in control of his creation, and who is working out all things for his glory and our good. When the world looks at us, may they see our peace instead of our problems, and be motivated to know the God who is the source of that peace. We pray these things in the name of our Lord and Savior, Jesus Christ. Amen."

Sharon opened her eyes, took a sip of lukewarm tea, and frowned involuntarily. Her family was going to come home soon, but they had two steps of *Lectio Divina* left. "After the Respond step comes the Rest step. This is where you pause and rest and let God speak to you. I like to approach it using the same attitude I've mentioned before, of Samuel inviting God to talk to him at night by saying, 'Speak, Lord, for your servant is listening.'"[61]

"So what do you actually *do* in this step?"

"Well, what *I* generally do is stop and ask God to speak to me on the basis of everything that has happened before, in all my reading and reflecting and praying about the passage in God's Word. This is the step that you can't rush because in a way this is the most important step, the step that all the other steps have been leading to, where we truly meet God in the Bible. So how about this. How about we remain silent for a few minutes, ask God to speak to us, and listen closely for what he has to say?"

Victoria nodded. "Sure, let's do that." The two women closed their eyes and prayed silently that God would speak to them from his Word. At first Victoria was distracted by her surroundings. The click of a clock on the wall. The hum of the refrigerator. The cars passing by outside. Then she became conscious of the fact that she was distracted and decided to intentionally focus on hearing the voice of God. "God, please speak to me from this passage," she prayed again silently. "What do you want me to learn, or to be, or to do?" She looked down at the passage in her Bible as a reminder. Yes, there was the obvious application to the situation with her mom, just as Sharon had prayed. She really *did* spend hours convulsed by worry, primarily that she would lose her mom to breast cancer. And she had recognized this before, and tried to give it over to God in prayer and claim his promise of peace. But was God trying to tell her something else too?

The more she looked at the passage and was reminded of what Sharon had done in the previous steps of *Lectio Divina*, the more she was convinced that God was also speaking to her from the second half of the passage, the one that talked about focusing on things that were true, honorable, pure, and lovely. Too much of her attention, she realized, was given over to things that simply did not fall into that category: to movies that were frivolous, or violent, or rude and profane; to music that glorified the bad instead of the good; to books that were at best mind candy and at worst dominated her thought life in negative ways; to television shows that were designed to shock or to appeal to the lowest common denominator of their audience. Before she became a Christian, she was a big partier and active in the club scene, and giving that up to spend time at church was a real lifestyle change for her. Now she realized that there were other changes in her life that were necessary in order to obey God's commands. "Thank you, God," she prayed in her mind. "Please give me the strength to change the focus of my life in other ways as well. And help me to find new things, positive things, to concentrate on instead."

Her eye moved down to the end of the passage and a thought occurred to her as she read that verse too. Maybe that's how God speaks to you, by bringing thoughts to your mind that are intended just for you while you are reading the Bible, she wondered. What drew her to this verse was something that Sharon had observed a few minutes earlier, that just as the apostle Paul had held himself up as a model for the church in Philippi, so too she was a model for her colleagues at work whether she wanted to be or not. They had been surprised and initially skeptical when she "found religion" (as they put it), and they continued to watch her to see if the changes in her life were real. "God," she prayed silently, "please help me to be an example of purity and peace to the people at work, especially to Sofía, who really needs your love and your power in her life right now. Please help her to trust you as her Savior."

Victoria looked over at Sharon and discovered that she was looking back. "Do you think you might be done with this step?" Sharon asked.

"I think so."

"Good. Let's talk about it, because I think the kids are just about to come home. How did God speak to you?"

Victoria summarized the ways she felt God might be speaking to her through the passage. "How about you, Sharon?" she inquired when she was finished.

"I was convicted about how much mindshare I've been giving to some of the political situations at church. Too often it consumes my thoughts and even keeps me from sleeping. I need to give it to God daily and walk in his peace and think about more positive things instead, like the fact that God distinctly called us here when we came several years ago. There's another verse in Philippians that gives me comfort that God is at work in my life and in control, no matter how challenging things look at the time. Here it is, in the first chapter of Philippians, verse 6: 'And I am sure of this, that he who began a good work in you will bring it to completion at the day of Jesus Christ.'[62]

"Oh," Sharon continued, "and just like you I was struck by Paul's role as a model to the Philippian church. As Josh's wife I am viewed as a model to our church as well, and need God's grace and strength so that I am a good model instead of a bad one. One of the ways I can serve as a good model is to be visibly gracious to the families who have chosen to leave. In fact, I think God is leading me to write a letter to the Johnsons telling them how grateful we were to have them in our church and to wish them well in their new church home."

Sharon mentally reviewed all that had happened that morning. "Victoria, you seemed to pick up on *Lectio Divina* really quickly. For many people the hardest steps are Reflect and Rest, because they're not used to slowing down, examining the text, engaging their imagination, and cultivating a conversation with God. There's one last step, the Act step, which I think we've pretty much already done. God seems to have been speaking to us throughout the entire *Lectio Divina* process about actions we need to take. By sharing those actions, as we've just done, we can hold each other accountable. Just be aware that in the Rest step God can also reveal deep truths about himself, or ourselves, or the world around us, not just actions or behavior changes that we need to make."

Since the kids were overdue and liable to return at any moment, Sharon summarized their time together. "What I've tried to provide this morning is an extended example of *Lectio Divina* for teaching purposes, to demonstrate the kinds of things that are possible. I've found that *Lectio Divina* is best learned by example; that's how Josh learned it from his friend in seminary, and that's the way he taught it to me. This is why I invited you to come over, because there's no way we could have done this realistically in the coffee shop. But when you do this at home it doesn't have to take as long or be as detailed as the way we did it this morning. Before the kids come home, let's pray and thank the Lord for our time together, shall we?"

The two women bowed their heads and Sharon led them in prayer. As she ended with "Amen" they heard the garage door open. Sharon looked up with a twinkle in her eye. The timing was perfect. Must have been a God Thing.

Short Version of *Lectio Divina* from Psalm 19

Victoria realized that she needed to try out *Lectio Divina* as soon as possible so that she could retain what she had just learned. So that evening she sat down with her Bible and a notebook to attempt a short version of *Lectio Divina* from Psalm 19, which Sharon suggested to her right before she left that morning. Victoria was getting better at remembering to use her notebook during her devotions; writing things down worked really well for her, and helped her not only to remember her insights but also to discover them in the first place.

She began by shooting off an arrow prayer from the Bible that she had learned from Sharon: "Speak, Lord, for your servant is listening."[63] Then she picked up her go-to Bible and turned to Psalm 19. The reason Sharon had suggested it was because Pastor Josh had recently preached a sermon from Psalm 19, and Sharon thought that practicing *Lectio Divina* from a passage that Victoria was familiar with might be a good way for her to learn how to do it by herself. She read it through several times slowly and out loud, so that she could involve as many senses as possible.

The heavens declare the glory of God,
  and the sky above proclaims his handiwork.
Day to day pours out speech,
  and night to night reveals knowledge.
There is no speech, nor are there words,
  whose voice is not heard.
Their voice goes out through all the earth,
  and their words to the end of the world.
In them he has set a tent for the sun,
    which comes out like a bridegroom leaving his chamber,
    and, like a strong man, runs its course with joy.
Its rising is from the end of the heavens,
    and its circuit to the end of them,
    and there is nothing hidden from its heat.
The law of the LORD is perfect,
    reviving the soul;
the testimony of the LORD is sure,
    making wise the simple;
the precepts of the LORD are right,
    rejoicing the heart;
the commandment of the LORD is pure,
    enlightening the eyes;
the fear of the LORD is clean,
    enduring forever;
the rules of the LORD are true,
    and righteous altogether.
More to be desired are they than gold,
    even much fine gold;
sweeter also than honey
    and drippings of the honeycomb.
Moreover, by them is your servant warned;
    in keeping them there is great reward.

> Who can discern his errors?
>> Declare me innocent from hidden faults.
> Keep back your servant also from presumptuous sins;
>> let them not have dominion over me!
> Then I shall be blameless,
>> and innocent of great transgression.
> Let the words of my mouth and the meditation of my heart
>> be acceptable in your sight,
>> O LORD, my rock and my redeemer.[64]

One of the things she remembered from Pastor Josh's sermon was that Psalm 19 was divided into three parts. She tried to recall what those parts were, and was helped by the spacing of the verses in her Bible. The first section[65] seemed to focus on God's creation; the second[66] on God's Word; and the third[67] on our response to God as he has revealed himself both in his creation and in his Word. Pastor Josh had called the first two sections "God's Book of Nature" and "God's Book of Scripture," because both of them revealed God but in different ways.

Taking a closer look at the psalm, Victoria noticed that the first section emphasizes how the power, glory, and majesty of God are revealed by his creation, and contains some wonderfully poetic imagery. The heavens, the sky, the day, and the night are personified as speaking the truth about their Creator. They are also described as a tent for the sun, which is pictured as a bridegroom leaving his marriage chamber or a strong man running his course with joy. That course traverses from one end of the heavens to the other, bathing everything in its heat. The second section stresses how God's Word reveals his perfection, his wisdom, his righteousness, his purity, and his truth. It too contains poetic imagery, and compares God's Word to gold and honey. Only now do human beings enter the picture, with the promise that God's

Word will serve as protection and reward. The third section gets very personal about how humans can never live up to the power and purity of God. Because of that, it implores God to protect against both unconscious and blatant sin so that thoughts and words were acceptable in God's sight. She couldn't help but relate those verses to the well-known phrase in the Lord's Prayer, "And lead us not into temptation, but deliver us from evil."[68] Victoria was also struck by the overall movement of the psalm: from God in his creation, to God in his Word, to humans in their sin, to humans in their plea for purity.

"OK, if I'm going to try a short version of *Lectio Divina*, that's probably enough for the Read step," she thought. Now for the Reflect step. A thought entered her mind, and she wondered if the psalm told the story of how someone learns about God. Well, maybe not *the* story, since many people learned about God from the love and words of their parents. But certainly *a* story about how God reveals himself to someone. Their first encounter with the glory of God and the immensity of his creation could easily have come from looking up at the sky. Victoria pictured someone lying outside at night, reveling in the milky white pinpricks that littered the heavens, and thrilling to the startlingly quick burnout of shooting stars. She remembered her first camping trip in high school, which provided her first extended experience of drinking in the night sky unobscured by light pollution. From the grandeur of the canopy of stars it is a short step to the glory of how night dissolves into day and back again. The immensity, the regularity, the healing warmth of the sun as it traces its great arc across the sky—each of these almost screams about the power and majesty of its Creator.

The generality of God's Book of Nature is completed by the specificity of God's Book of Scripture. Victoria pictured the same person who stayed awake outdoors entranced by the stars picking up a Bible the next day to learn about the One who created the stars, and discovering God's holiness, purity, righteousness, and wisdom embedded in the commands of Scripture. Those commands were all over the Bible; Victoria had found them in the Law of Moses, in the proverbs of Solomon, in the words of Jesus, and in the letters of the apostle Paul. But those commands were never arbitrary; instead, they were always grounded in the character of God as Creator who knows what is best for his creation. If God knows how to set the stars in the sky and make day follow night, he also knows how his human creatures can live in harmony both with him and with each other.

Then Victoria imagined that person reading the Bible becoming very uncomfortable as they realized how far short they fell from the holiness that God expects from his creatures. This realization would inevitably lead them to cry out to God for help. Those cries for help would ideally culminate in putting their trust in Jesus as their Savior, because help was only possible by the power of God on the basis of Jesus' sacrifice on the cross. But help was needed every *other* time that person encountered God through his Word and realized that their life still fell short of the righteousness of God. The cry of their heart would be that God would purge them of sins known and unknown, and render them blameless and acceptable in his sight. This cycle—from the glory of God, to the holiness of God, to their own unholiness, to their cry for help—would continue for as long as they lived.

She finished writing her meditations in her notebook. Time to transition to the Response step and pray Scripture back to God. She kept her eyes and her Bible open. "God," she prayed aloud, "the heavens declare your glory, and the sky proclaims that you made it. Day and night tell the story of your creation to everyone who will listen, and serve as a tent for the sun, who runs his race each day radiating joy and heat. Your Book of Scripture reveals who you are just like your Book of Nature does, and demonstrates that you are perfect, trustworthy, wise, righteous, pure, clean, and true, just like gold and honey. These truths warn and reward us, because we are full of sin both known and unknown. God, declare us—declare *me*—innocent of hidden faults, and do not let presumptuous sins have dominion over me. Lead me not into temptation so that I can be blameless and innocent of great transgression. Let the words of my mouth and the meditation of my heart be acceptable in your sight, O Lord, my rock and my redeemer." She wrote an observation in her notebook about how easy it was to pray Scripture when the words were already a prayer.

Now it was time to Rest, to be silent in God's presence and listen for his voice speaking to her personally from the Bible. She scanned the passage again and was struck by how little time she actually spent out in nature. She'd always been a city girl, and her family never did much outdoors, just an occasional picnic in a park on a holiday. Maybe she needed to spend more time learning about God in his creation. Learning about God in the Bible was another story, however. Pretty much every time she read it, she came away painfully aware that her life fell far short from what God expected. Especially in the area of hidden faults, the sins she wasn't even aware of until the Bible opened her eyes to them. Or her family or somebody at work. That last verse really nailed it for her: "Let the words of my mouth and the meditation of my heart be acceptable in your sight."[69] Too often the words of her mouth were petty or rude, especially at work, generally by reaction instead of intentional action, which was really no excuse. And if she were honest with herself it all began with the thoughts and meditations of her heart, because she often found herself thinking, "Did I just say that out loud?" Maybe if she spent more time focusing on what God had revealed about himself, in nature and in Scripture, it would transform not just her thoughts but also her speech.

The Act step was the final one in the process. Victoria wondered if she could figure out an "R" word to remember it with, so she racked her brain for something suitable. "Reify," perhaps? She smiled; at least her English major was good for something, not just for becoming an educated taxi driver like her brothers always teased. "OK, focus," she told herself. How could she put into practice what she had just heard from God in Psalm 19? Maybe she could take a hike in the woods sometime on a day off. But definitely she should continue to read the Bible and pray for God's help in living a holy life, especially when it came to her thoughts and words. And since Sharon had been encouraging her to memorize Scripture, she thought she'd work up to memorizing all of Psalm 19 by beginning with the last verse, because it was such a useful prayer: "Let the words of my mouth and the meditation of my heart be acceptable in your sight, O Lord, my rock and my redeemer."[70]

Victoria turned that last verse into a final prayer that she spoke out loud. Then she closed her Bible, rose from the couch, and went into the bathroom of her small apartment to get ready for bed.

BIBLICAL INTERPRETATION:
HOW TO DISCERN GOD'S VOICE

"So how do I know that it is really God who is speaking to me through the Bible?" Victoria asked with a frown. She absentmindedly twirled her hair with her index finger. "I mean, after I concentrate hard on the passage and then try to listen to God in silence, how do I know that it is God who is speaking to me and not just my own thoughts, or worse, the devil trying to manipulate my mind?"

Sharon smiled knowingly, both because this was an issue that she had wrestled with herself and because it had come up in every discipleship relationship that she had been involved in. "Wow, great questions. And what you are really asking are two separate but related questions. One is how to discern God's voice. The other is how to interpret the Bible. Let me address the last one first and then circle back." She paused to figure out the best way to proceed. "I'll start by highlighting what the Bible says about itself. One of the single best verses for this comes from the book of Second Peter. I'll find it for us." Sharon tapped on her phone and then read aloud 2 Peter 1:21. "'For no prophecy was ever produced by the will of man, but men spoke from God as they were carried along by the Holy Spirit.'[71] The apostle Peter was talking about prophecies of the coming of Christ in particular, but what he said applies to the Bible in general. And we learn at least two things from this verse. First, the Bible has *two* authors, a human author and a divine author. Second, the human author was given this revelation from God for a particular purpose and in a particular context, a particular historical time and place."

Victoria looked somewhat puzzled. "How did that actually work? I mean, how can something have two authors?"

"The actual mechanics are a mystery, and for the most part it doesn't appear that God was *dictating* words to the human authors. Perhaps the best way to understand it, which is consistent with the verse I just read, is that the Holy Spirit guided the writing process so that the words of the human author were also the words of God."

Sharon stopped because the barista who always greeted them by name was making a drink for a drive-in customer and waved to them from behind the counter. She waved back and went on. "Most of the biblical interpretation principles that I'm about to tell you are grounded in the fact that the Bible was revealed by God to humans in context. The biblical authors were living in a particular historical and geographical context, and their words were embedded in a literary context. The principle that I should probably start with is to be aware of the kind of literature the human author was writing and interpret what the author is saying in a way that is consistent with that kind of literature. You were an English major, so you know what I mean when I call that the literary genre."

Victoria grinned. "I do indeed."

"Well, the Bible contains a lot of those literary genres. Historical narrative, poetry, law, letters, parables, gospels, prophecy, proverbs. And each one has different conventions for how it should be interpreted. For example, when we read in the Psalms that the rivers should clap their hands and the mountains should sing,[72] we know that the psalmist was not speaking literally because he was writing poetry. But when we read something in the Law, we can generally assume that the writer was speaking directly and literally. When Josh teaches a biblical interpretation class during Sunday School at church, he starts off by identifying the literary genres in the Bible and then develops interpretation conventions that apply to each genre."

"How can I get a list of these interpretation conventions?"

"Let me send you a link to some good books that focus on a genre-based approach to interpreting the Bible. This approach used to be taught mostly in college or seminary, but some really good resources are now available for lay people."

Sharon thought for a moment. "A second principle is to interpret a passage in the Bible not just according to its literary *genre* but also in its literary *context*. Do you recall ever reading in the newspaper that someone has accused a reporter of taking them out of context? Well, we need to make sure that we don't do the same thing to the biblical writers. We need to consider *all* of the wider contexts when we interpret something in the Bible, from the context of the enclosing sentence on up: the enclosing paragraph, the enclosing section, the enclosing book, and even larger contexts. Interpretation should be *consistent* with its context, not *different* from its context. A third principle—I'm at number three, right? —is also contextual, which is to take into account the historical and geographical context of the author when we interpret what they wrote. For example, knowing that the author of Revelation is speaking to a persecuted church, or that the apostle Paul wrote Philippians from prison, goes a long way toward helping us understand what they are saying. A fourth principle is to consider the intent and purpose of the author in writing what they did; an interpretation that varies widely from the original intent of the author is generally not a valid one. When he was in seminary, Josh had a professor who would frequently say, 'It cannot mean what it never meant.' I don't know that I agree with that in *all* cases, but it's a pretty good rule of thumb. An exception to this rule is that you also need to consider the intent of the *divine* author, which always builds upon but sometimes transcends the intent of the human author. Prophecies or foreshadowings of the coming of Christ can fall into this category. A prophet might have spoken about the coming of Christ using the words or limited understanding that God revealed to him, but God knew the fuller meaning of what was being said and generally unfolded it later on in Scripture."

Victoria had a flash of insight. "So what you're telling me is that if I encounter something in my Quiet Time that is difficult to understand, I may need to read more widely in the Bible in order to interpret it properly."

"Exactly. And this can take a bit of time, so you may not be able to address it during your Quiet Time itself, but instead have to defer it until later."

Sharon finished her tea. "There are several more-specialized principles of biblical interpretation that are useful in certain situations, but let me end with a couple that I find particularly helpful in general. Use Scripture itself to interpret Scripture. Meaning, if you read something in Scripture and are not quite sure what it means, look up similar passages in Scripture and try to interpret them all together. Of course, it's best if you start with similar passages in the same book, or by the same author, or from the same time period, or from the same literary genre, before casting your net wider. Related to that principle is that you want to use the clear passages in Scripture to help you understand the less clear—or even obscure—passages of Scripture. Let me give you a couple of examples. Do you recall hearing in the news from time to time that some group has interpreted the symbolic language in Revelation in a particular way and set a date for the end of the world? If only they would have interpreted those obscure symbols in light of the clear statement by Jesus that no one knows the day or the hour of his return![73] Or—and I get this more often than you might think—somebody will come up to me absolutely terrified that they might have blasphemed against the Holy Spirit and lost their salvation, which Jesus himself warns against.[74] But they haven't taken into account the very clear Scriptures that state that the Holy Spirit has sealed us and protected us for the day of redemption.[75] Besides, the very fact that someone is afraid of having blasphemed against the Holy Spirit is generally a sign that they haven't done that at all; it's the ones who have no such fear and whose lives show a clear pattern of rebellion against God that need to be worried."

"How can I find Scripture passages that are related to the one I am reading so that I can let Scripture interpret Scripture?"

"Well, there's a bunch of ways to do that. You can always look up your passage in a Bible handbook or commentary to see what other Scripture passages are mentioned. But perhaps the easiest way is to check out the Scripture cross-references in your Bible or on your phone. You'll need to get a Bible or an app that includes cross-references, though. You could also buy a study Bible and read the notes on that passage. But if you can, you'd be wise to look at *several* study Bibles to get multiple points of view, not just one. Same thing with Bible commentaries."

Sharon looked directly at Victoria. "Not everybody agrees with what I'm about to say, but I believe there are times when the Holy Spirit, as the divine author of Scripture, will take a passage and apply it directly to our lives in ways that go beyond the intent of the human author of Scripture. I think you need to be careful when that happens, but I think you need to be open to it as well. Here's an example. Several years ago, Josh came down with a mysterious medical condition where the symptoms were muscle weakness in his arms and legs. We took him from doctor to doctor and all they could do was guess, because the objective measures like MRIs and his blood work kept coming back normal. Then one day Josh was reading through Isaiah and a verse jumped out and spoke to him. Let me see if I can remember what it was." Sharon used the search feature of the Bible app on her phone to see if she could find it. After a couple of false starts she cried out, "Oh, here it is! Isaiah 35, verse 3. 'Strengthen the weak hands, and make firm the feeble knees.'[76] Even though Isaiah was addressing the exiles of the nation of Israel and promising them that they would someday return, and even though the verse was actually a command, Josh took it as a *promise* from God directly to him that his weak hands and legs would one day be strengthened. And for him it was a real comfort. It took a couple of years, but that's exactly what happened; Josh eventually recovered. We still have no real idea of what was going on medically, but for Josh that verse was a turning point spiritually and emotionally. The way Josh talks about it now is that he believes God spoke to him through Scripture in a way that transcended the original context, but that you have to be cautious when that occurs. First, you have to make sure that you apply that word only to yourself, not to everybody else. Second, you have to suspend final judgment until sufficient time has passed to validate whether the promise actually comes true. In his case it did."

Because she could read some confusion on Victoria's face, Sharon expanded her explanation. "Let me give you another example. Do you remember when our church hosted a Refugee Night with all those refugee agencies in town?"

Victoria shook her head. "I wanted to go but I spent the evening with my mom instead."

"Oh, I'm sorry; I thought I saw you there. Anyway, one of the refugees from a country in Africa gave her testimony that night. I was fascinated, because the same kind of thing happened to her that happened to Josh. Her country was devastated by war and members of her family were killed. The situation was really dire and her future was bleak. Then a verse in the book of Exodus seemed to reach out and grab her; I'll find it and read it for you." Sharon tapped on her phone several times. "Ah, Exodus 23, verse 20. 'Behold, I send an angel before you to guard you on the way and to bring you to the place that I have prepared.'[77] Moses was speaking these words from God to the Israelites in the wilderness as a promise that God would lead them to the Promised Land. But the woman who spoke to us interpreted it as a promise from God directly to *her*, that God would lead her from her war-torn country into another country in which she could live in safety and peace. And over time, that's exactly what happened. She clung to that verse as a special word from God during the entire process."

Victoria pondered what Sharon had said. "I don't think something like that has ever happened to me; at least not yet."

"I understand. I just wanted to mention it in case it ever does." Sharon mentally switched gears. "We can now circle back to your first question, which is how to discern God's voice in the Bible. There are several principles at play here as well." She ticked the principles off on her fingers. "If it is truly God's voice then it will generally be related to the passage you have read in some way and will not be just a random thought that has crossed your mind. If it is truly God's voice it will never contradict any of God's other words in the Bible. If it is truly God's voice it will most likely be consistent with the clear words of God in Scripture instead of the obscure ones. If it is truly God's voice then what you hear will apply directly to you and your situation, and yield results that are for your good and God's glory. If it is truly God's voice then generally the Church—other believers that you know and trust—will affirm that it is God's voice as well. If it is truly God's voice then it will stand the test of time. Finally, as you get to know God better, your ability to distinguish what is actually God's voice from what is *not* God's voice will improve. This happens in every relationship; for example, as our own friendship has deepened over time, hasn't it become easier to understand me and to figure out what I am saying?" Victoria nodded her head affirmatively. "So ... do these principles make sense and address your questions?" Sharon concluded.

"I think so. I mean, I'll need to get more experience with this. But what you say *does* make sense, and gives me more confidence that the voice I am hearing might actually be God instead of something else. Thanks!" She looked around at the coffee shop, which was now almost empty.

"Can I pray for us before we go home?" Sharon asked, suddenly aware of the time. Victoria nodded. Sharon bowed her head. "Heavenly Father, your Son said in your Word that his sheep hear his voice, and that he knows them as their shepherd.[78] Lord, give each of us a spirit of discernment, and eyes to see and ears to hear when it is truly you who is speaking to us in the Bible. Protect each of us from our own random thoughts and from our Enemy, who wants to influence and control our minds. And may we not just hear your voice but also put into practice what you are telling us to do and to be. We pray these things in the name of your Son, our Lord and Savior, Jesus Christ. Amen."

CONCLUSION

PUTTING ENCOUNTER INTO PRACTICE

Our story about Victoria and Sharon has come to an end, at least for now. My hope is that by allowing you to listen in on a realistic discipleship process, and to follow each character as they meet God in his Word in the midst of the joys and messiness of everyday life, you too will have learned ways to enhance your own encounters with God. In the extended story above, three major approaches to devotional reading of the Bible have been presented: Quiet Time, Spiritual Journaling, and *Lectio Divina*. Along the way, other important Spiritual Formation practices—such as prayer, Scripture memorization, overcoming temptation, and biblical interpretation—were modeled as well.

Throughout the book the stress has been on the Bible as a portal through which we meet God and are changed by the experience. The Bible itself tells us that it was designed by God to function that way. The apostle Paul reveals the source and purpose of Scripture in these words to Timothy, his *protégé* and "son in the faith":[79]

> But as for you, continue in what you have learned and have firmly believed, knowing from whom you learned it and how from childhood you have been acquainted with the sacred writings, which are able to make you wise for salvation through faith in Christ Jesus. All Scripture is breathed out by God and profitable for teaching, for reproof, for correction, and for training in righteousness, that the man of God may be complete, equipped for every good work.[80]

At times that encounter with God will be glorious. But at other times that experience of the presence of God will be uncomfortable, as the author of Hebrews attests:

> For the word of God is living and active, sharper than any two-edged sword, piercing to the division of soul and of spirit, of joints and of marrow, and discerning the thoughts and intentions of the heart. And no creature is hidden from his sight, but all are naked and exposed to the eyes of him to whom we must give account.[81]

In the Bible, the nature, character, and heart of God are revealed, which of necessity illuminates the nature and character of our own heart and the brokenness of the world around us. But just as this book has emphasized that reading the Bible does not end with the head, so too it does not end with the heart. Unless the hands are involved, and action is taken to put into practice what the head has learned and the heart has experienced, the encounter with God is incomplete.

May God's story intersect with your own story and positively impact the story of your world. Head, heart, and hands. Blessings!

FURTHER READING

Alexander, David and Pat, eds. *Zondervan Handbook to the Bible.* 5th ed. Grand Rapids, MI: Zondervan, 2018. An extremely popular and well-illustrated Bible handbook. Consider it an indispensable companion as you read your way through the Bible.

Carson, D. A. *Praying with Paul: A Call to Spiritual Reformation.* Grand Rapids, MI: Baker Academic, 1992, 2014. How to use the prayers of the apostle Paul as pedagogy in the School of Prayer.

Cepero, Helen. *Journaling as a Spiritual Practice: Encountering God through Attentive Writing.* Downers Grove, IL: InterVarsity Press, 2008. A thoughtful discussion of the practice of Spiritual Journaling in general.

Cordeiro, Wayne. *The Divine Mentor: Growing Your Faith as You Sit at the Feet of the Savior.* Minneapolis, MN: Bethany House, 2007. A detailed description of the SOAP method of Spiritual Journaling by its creator.

Fleming, Jean. *Feeding Your Soul: A Quiet Time Handbook.* Colorado Springs, CO: NavPress, 1999. A comprehensive and well-regarded handbook about how to practice a lifelong habit of a regular Quiet Time.

Fee, Gordon D., and Douglas Stuart. *How to Read the Bible for All Its Worth*. 4th Edition. Grand Rapids, MI: Zondervan, 2014. A time-tested, genre-based introduction to interpreting the Bible.

Foster, Richard J. *Prayer: Finding the Heart's True Home*. San Francisco, CA: HarperSanFrancisco, 1992. A helpful catalog and discussion of a full spectrum of prayer methods.

Gray, Tim. *Praying Scripture for a Change: An Introduction to Lectio Divina*. West Chester, PA: Ascension Press, 2009. An excellent, Word-based introduction to *Lectio Divina* from a Roman Catholic perspective.

InterVarsity Staff. *Quiet Time: A Practical Guide for Daily Devotions*. Revised Edition. Downers Grove, IL: InterVarsity Press, 1976. First published in 1945, this booklet popularized the practice of a Quiet Time among Protestant Evangelicals in the English-speaking world.

Johnson, Jan. *Meeting God in Scripture: A Hands-On Guide to Lectio Divina*. Downers Grove, IL: IVP Books, 2016. A set of devotions to walk an individual or a group through *Lectio Divina*.

Lawrence, Brother. *The Practice of the Presence of God*. Available in several editions, both online and in print. A classic description of how to sustain a prayer connection with God throughout the day, no matter how humble the activity being performed.

Longman III, Tremper, ed. *The Baker Illustrated Bible Dictionary*. Grand Rapids, MI: Baker Books, 2013. An illustrated dictionary of the major topics, terms, and names in the Bible. Part of the three-volume *Baker Illustrated Bible* set, which includes a dictionary, a handbook, and a commentary.

Mathewes-Green, Frederica. *The Jesus Prayer: The Ancient Desert Prayer that Tunes the Heart to God.* Brewster, MA: Paraclete Press, 2009. Presents the theology and practice of the Jesus Prayer from an Eastern Orthodox perspective.

Reinders, Philip F. *Seeking God's Face: Praying with the Bible through the Year.* Grand Rapids, MI: Faith Alive Christian Resources, 2010, 2012. Scripture readings for each day of the liturgical year, with a focus on reflection, prayer, and listening to God's voice.

Whitney, Donald S. *Spiritual Disciplines for the Christian Life.* Revised and Updated. Colorado Springs, CO: NavPress, 1991, 2014. The source of some of the Bible reading plan recommendations.

————. *Praying the Bible.* Wheaton, IL: Crossway, 2015. Though the terms are not explicitly mentioned, this book can be used to provide a comprehensive framework for the Reflect step of *Lectio Divina.*

Wilhoit, James C., and Evan B. Howard. *Discovering Lectio Divina: Bringing Scripture into Ordinary Life.* Downers Grove, IL: InterVarsity Press, 2012. A solid, application-focused discussion of *Lectio Divina* from a Protestant Evangelical perspective.

STUDY GUIDE

Introduction

1. Do you currently practice a regular Quiet Time? If so, how frequently and for about how long each time? If not, what might be keeping you from having a regular Quiet Time?

2. Assuming that you've had some experience with Quiet Times, what do you actually *do* during a typical Quiet Time? Describe one from beginning to end. What questions do you use to guide your devotional reading of the passage?

3. Which questions did Sharon recommend that Victoria ask during her Quiet Time? Using those questions, practice a Quiet Time in a passage of your choice either alone or in a group.

4. How did you come to know Jesus as your Savior? Did someone play a similar role in your life that Jennifer played in Victoria's? Has someone played a similar discipleship role in your life that Sharon is playing in Victoria's? Have *you* played a similar role to Jennifer or Sharon in someone else's life?

Chapter One

1. Do you struggle with the tendency to read Scripture academically instead of devotionally? If so, what has helped you to approach Scripture more devotionally and practically instead of just academically?

2. What does "meeting God in the Bible" mean to you in practical terms?

3. What steps can you take to make it more likely that you actually put into practice what you have learned during your encounter with God in a Quiet Time?

4. To what extent does your own heart resonate with the psalmist when he exclaims, "Oh how I love your law! It is my meditation all the day."?[82] Do you meditate on Scripture as well? If so, how do you do it?

Chapter Two

1. Which Quiet Time scheduling practices have worked well for you? Which practices have not worked out so well? If you are new to Quiet Times, which scheduling practices do you *think* might work well for you, or might not work out so well?

2. How many verses do you usually focus on during your Quiet Times, or do you *think* you should focus on during your Quiet Times? Which considerations might affect the number of verses that you choose?

3. Assuming that you've had some experience with Quiet Times, how frequently do your Quiet Times get interrupted? How often are you able to finish what you have

started? Which habits or practices have helped you either to avoid interruptions or to finish Quiet Times that have been interrupted?

4. Either alone or in a group, practice a Quiet Time from another passage in the Gospel of John, such as Jesus' meeting with Nicodemus in John 3:1-21, Jesus' healing of the blind man in John 9, or Jesus' High Priestly Prayer in John 17. Note that one of the first decisions you will want to make is the size of the passage to focus on in your Quiet Time.

Chapter Three

1. If someone asked you to give your spiritual testimony, what would you say?

2. Has the way that you use or regard Scripture changed over time? If so, describe those changes.

3. Have you ever experienced a crisis that brought you closer both to God and to his Word? If so, to the extent that you are comfortable, discuss that crisis and how it affected you spiritually.

4. How would you evaluate your spiritual life right now? What is going well? What do you wish were going better? How might those wishes become reality?

Chapter Four

1. In what ways was Sharon's Quiet Time in chapter four different from Victoria's Quiet Time in chapter two? In what ways were they similar?

2.   How did God's Prescription for Mental Health in Philippians 4:4–9 speak to your own current situation?

3.   Sharon identified a number of ways that she could apply the lessons of her passage. What would you recommend that Sharon do to make it more likely that she *will* apply those lessons to her life? Which of those recommendations might you find helpful yourself, and why?

4.   Either alone or in a group, practice an application-focused Quiet Time like Sharon did in one of the following passages of Scripture: Psalm 8; Psalm 23; Psalm 51; Ecclesiastes 3:1–8; Matthew 5:2–11; Romans 12:1–8; Ephesians 4:25–32; James 1:2–8.

Chapter Five

1.   How has your own Quiet Time changed since you began reading this book?

2.   Which version of the Bible do you find yourself using most often in your Quiet Times? How would you characterize it? How do you like it? If you use a combination of versions, which combination works best for you, and why?

3.   How does ACTS Prayer compare to the Lord's Prayer, which is the model prayer that Jesus taught his disciples?[83] Which component of an ACTS Prayer do you find yourself praying the most often? If your own prayers are not balanced, how might they be rebalanced?

4.   Either alone or in a group, compose an ACTS Prayer for a Quiet Time based on the same passage of Scripture you chose for question four in the previous chapter: Psalm 8; Psalm 23; Psalm 51; Ecclesiastes 3:1–8; Matthew 5:2–11;

Romans 12:1–8; Ephesians 4:25–32; James 1:2–8. Divide it into two sections, the "AC" part to begin the Quiet Time and the "TS" part to end it.

Chapter Six

1. Victoria used Psalm 150 as a model for creating a prayer of adoration to start off an ACTS Prayer. Which other models of adoration in Scripture have you found helpful? Starter suggestion: Revelation 4:8b, 11.

2. Which models of thanksgiving in Scripture have you found helpful? Starter suggestion: Psalm 106:1–2.

3. Which models of confession in Scripture have you found helpful? Starter suggestions: Psalm 32:1–7; Psalm 38.

4. Which models of supplication in Scripture have you found helpful? Starter suggestion: Ephesians 1:15–23.

5. In general, which book of the Bible would you expect to be a rich source of prayer models?

Chapter Seven

1. Compose a complete standalone ACTS Prayer based on what is currently going on in your life. If you are in a group, share it with the group to the extent that you feel comfortable.

2. Have you ever used a Bible reading plan? If so, describe your experience. Which one(s) did you choose? What has worked for you? What hasn't worked so well? How have you been able to balance following a Bible reading

plan in which you learn more about Scripture with having a Quiet Time in which you truly encounter God?

3. If you haven't used a Bible reading plan, how do you select the passages of Scripture for your Quiet Times? Which passages of Scripture or books of the Bible have you focused on in your Quiet Times so far? Which passages or books are you planning to focus on in the future, and why?

4. Which Bible verses might be particularly appropriate to use to begin and end your Quiet Times with prayer?

Chapter Eight

1. Have you ever committed Scripture to memory? If so, describe your experience. What has worked for you? What hasn't worked so well? Which Scripture passages have you already memorized? In what situations has the Holy Spirit brought them back to your mind when they were needed? If you are in a group, share those experiences with the group to the extent that you are comfortable.

2. Which favorite passages of Scripture would you like to commit to memory? Which memory strategies might be most appropriate for each of those passages?

3. Identify appropriate memory strategies for one of the following passages of Scripture: Psalm 8; Psalm 23; Psalm 51; Ecclesiastes 3:1–8; Matthew 5:2–11; Romans 12:1–8; Ephesians 4:25–32; James 1:2–8.

4. Begin the process of memorizing Philippians 4:4–9 yourself, whether alone or in a group.

Chapter Nine

1. What is the purpose of each step of the SOAP method of Spiritual Journaling? Compare and contrast Spiritual Journaling with the way the book describes a Quiet Time. How does it compare with Quiet Times as *you* have practiced them?

2. In what ways might you be able to integrate ACTS Prayer into the practice of Spiritual Journaling?

3. Do you currently use a notebook or journal during your Quiet Times? If so, what kinds of things do you record in your journal? If not, why not?

4. Based on the passage in Matthew 4:1–11, how might the practices of devotional reading of Scripture and Bible memorization help you to overcome temptation? How have you experienced victory over temptation using Scripture as a weapon in your own life? If you are in a group, share one of those experiences to the extent that you are comfortable.

5. Pick one of the following passages of Scripture to practice the SOAP method of Spiritual Journaling, either alone or in a group: Psalm 8; Psalm 23; Psalm 51; Ecclesiastes 3:1–8; Matthew 5:2–11; Romans 12:1–8; Ephesians 4:25–32; James 1:2–8.

Chapter Ten

1. Identify appropriate memory strategies for another of the following passages of Scripture: Psalm 8; Psalm 23; Psalm 51; Ecclesiastes 3:1–8; Matthew 5:2–11; Romans 12:1–8; Ephesians 4:25–32; James 1:2–8.

2. Create a song or a rhythm to help you memorize Philippians 4:4–9.

3. Create a unifying image, or a unified set of mental images, or a mnemonic device (such as an acronym or an acrostic) to help you memorize Philippians 4:4–9. Which other memorization strategies might be useful?

4. Complete the process of memorizing Philippians 4:4–9 yourself, whether alone or in a group. Pray that the Holy Spirit might bring it to mind sometime this week when it is needed.

Chapter Eleven

1. In what ways was Victoria's Quiet Time from Psalm 91 different than other Quiet Times described in the book up to this point? How has your own emotional state affected how you approach Scripture in your Quiet Times, if at all?

2. Which passages of Scripture have you clung to during crises in your life? If you are in a group, to the extent you feel comfortable, describe a time of crisis in your life and a Scripture passage that especially spoke to you during that crisis.

3. Which memory strategies might you use to memorize Psalm 91?

4. Practice the SOAP method of Spiritual Journaling using Psalm 91.

Chapter Twelve

1. Though she didn't describe it in those terms, in this chapter Sharon articulated a Trinitarian theology of prayer. In

your own words, summarize that theology and its scriptural foundations. How is each member of the Godhead involved both in the act of prayer and in the answering of prayer?

2. In what ways have you attempted to obey the command to "pray without ceasing"[84] in your own life? What other ways of obeying this command are you aware of, both in the lives of people you know and in Christian traditions throughout history? If this is new to you, what ways of obeying this command do you *think* might work for you?

3. Reflect on the contrast that Sharon offered between prayer as event and prayer as state. In what ways for you is prayer an event? In what ways for you is prayer a state? How might prayer become more of a state than an event for you?

4. Describe the motivation for and scriptural basis of the Jesus Prayer. How and in what situations might the Jesus Prayer be helpful in your own life?

Chapter Thirteen

1. Review the steps of *Lectio Divina*, including the optional ones. What takes place in each step?

2. How does *Lectio Divina* compare to the way that a Quiet Time and Spiritual Journaling were described in the book? What might be the advantages or disadvantages of *Lectio Divina* compared to those other devotional Bible study methods?

3. Have you ever performed *Lectio Divina* before? If so, what did you think of it? If not, how comfortable do you think you might be with the Reflect and Rest steps?

4.   How might the optional steps of Prepare and Act (and even Record) be useful in the *Lectio Divina* process?

Chapter Fourteen

1.   Compare and contrast the Read step of *Lectio Divina* with the three questions that the book suggests for a Quiet Time.

2.   Compare and contrast the Read step of *Lectio Divina* with the Observation step of the SOAP method of Spiritual Journaling.

3.   How might the use of a notebook or additional Bible translations help you in the Read step?

4.   Practice the Read step using one of the following passages of Scripture that you have not studied in a previous chapter: Psalm 8; Psalm 23; Psalm 51; Ecclesiastes 3:1–8; Matthew 5:2–11; Romans 12:1–8; Ephesians 4:25–32; James 1:2–8.

Chapter Fifteen

1.   In your own words, describe what happens in the Reflect step of *Lectio Divina*. How does it relate to the preceding step, the Read step? Other than visualization, which other ways to meditate on the passage might be useful?

2.   Which visualization perspectives in the chapter resonated with you the most? Which resonated with you the least?

3.   How could the Reflect step be used to help you memorize Scripture?

4.   Practice the Reflect step using the same passage of Scripture you chose in the last question for the previous chapter.

Chapter Sixteen

1.   In your own words, describe what happens in the Respond, Rest, and Act steps of *Lectio Divina*. How does each step relate to the step that precedes it?
2.   Does the Respond step of *Lectio Divina* have a direct counterpart either in the way the book describes a Quiet Time or in the SOAP method of Spiritual Journaling?
3.   The Rest and Act steps in *Lectio Divina* correspond to which steps in the way the book describes a Quiet Time and in the SOAP method of Spiritual Journaling?
4.   Practice the Respond, Rest, and Act steps using the same passage of Scripture you focused on in the last question for the previous chapter.

Chapter Seventeen

1.   How did the short version of *Lectio Divina* that Victoria practiced in this chapter differ from the version that Sharon led her through in the previous chapters?
2.   Compose an ACTS Prayer based on Psalm 19. How might the psalm itself make it relatively easy to do this?
3.   Which memory strategies might be most appropriate for memorizing Psalm 19?
4.   Practice a short version of *Lectio Divina* using one of the following passages of Scripture that you have not yet chosen: Psalm 8; Psalm 23; Psalm 51; Ecclesiastes 3:1–8;

Matthew 5:2–11; Romans 12:1–8; Ephesians 4:25–32; James 1:2–8.

Chapter Eighteen

1. List the general principles of biblical interpretation that Sharon explained to Victoria. Are there other interpretation principles that you have used in your own Bible study?

2. Which literary genre in the Bible do you find yourself spending the most time reading? Which special interpretation conventions might apply to that genre?

3. List the criteria for discerning God's voice that Sharon passed on to Victoria. Are there other criteria that you have used to determine whether it is really God who is speaking to you from the Bible?

4. Have you ever had an experience like those that Sharon described, in which God spoke to you directly from Scripture in ways that went beyond the original context? If you are in a group, to the extent that you are comfortable, describe the situation and the passage of Scripture, and tell the story of what happened over time.

Conclusion

1. How has your practice of reading Scripture devotionally and meeting God in the Bible changed by reading this book? Which of the devotional Bible study methods (Quiet Time, Spiritual Journaling, *Lectio Divina*) did you find useful in meeting God, and why? Did they complement each other in any way?

2.   What have you learned about prayer, Bible memoriza-
      tion, overcoming temptation, biblical interpretation,
      and the discipleship process that you found helpful?

3.   Pick one of the well-known passages about the Bible in
      this chapter and identify an appropriate memorization
      strategy for it. Resolve to commit that passage to
      memory this week.

4.   What steps will you take going forward to ensure that
      you truly meet God when you read the Bible devotion-
      ally, and that you obey his voice by putting into practice
      what he tells you to do?

Appendix 1

Topic Summaries

Quiet Time Questions

1. What does this passage tell me about God?
2. What does this passage tell me about myself?
3. With God's help, how should my life be changed so that I can become more like God?

Bible Translations

1. Primary translations: English Standard Version (ESV) and New International Version (NIV). A roughly equivalent pairing for Spanish Bible translations is La Biblia de las Américas (LBLA) and Nueva Versión Internacional (NVI).
2. Secondary translations: New Living Translation (NLT) and Christian Standard Bible (CSB).

Spiritual Journaling using the SOAP Method

1. Scripture
2. Observation
3. Application
4. Prayer

Lectio Divina

1.   (Optional) Prepare: Generally an opening prayer or a brief Scripture reading. The Latin name for this step is *Praeparatio* (pree-pah-**rah**-tee-oh).

2.   Read: Read the passage through several times, slowly and out loud. Observe themes and connections. Do a mini Bible study. The Latin name for this step is *Lectio* (**lek**-tee-oh).

3.   Reflect (or Ruminate): Meditate on the passage. Unleash your imagination and visualize the text from multiple perspectives. The Latin name for this step is *Meditatio* (meh-di-**tah**-tee-oh).

4.   Respond: Pray the passage back to God. The Latin name for this step is *Oratio* (oh-**rah**-tee-oh).

5.   Rest (or Receive): Wait in silence for God's voice, for God to meet you in the passage. The Latin name for this step is *Contemplatio* (con-tem-**plah**-tee-oh).

6.   (Optional) Act: Apply the passage to your life through changes in actions and attitudes. The Latin name for this step is *Actio* (**act**-tee-oh).

ACTS Prayer

1.   Adoration
2.   Confession
3.   Thanksgiving
4.   Supplication

The Jesus Prayer

"Lord Jesus Christ, Son of God, have mercy on me, a sinner."

How to Memorize Scripture

1. Post the verse in a prominent location, such as on the refrigerator, so that you can be constantly reminded of it.
2. Commit to memory by brute force (*i.e.*, a continuous cycle of recite-and-check), perhaps using flash cards.
3. Create an acronym, an acrostic, or a summary phrase to help you remember.
4. Create a song or a rhythm to help you remember.
5. Create a unifying mental image or a series of mental images to help you remember.

Biblical Interpretation Principles

1. Be aware of the kind of literature (literary genre) the human author was writing and interpret what the author is saying in a way that is consistent with that kind of literature.
2. Interpret a passage in the Bible not just according to its literary *genre* but also in its literary *context*.
3. Take into account the historical and geographical context of the author.
4. Consider the intent and purpose of the author in writing what they did; an interpretation that varies widely from the original intent of the author is generally not a valid one.
5. Take into account the intent of the *divine* author as well.
6. Use Scripture itself to interpret Scripture.
7. Use the clear passages in Scripture to help you understand the less clear, or even obscure, passages of Scripture.

How to Discern God's Voice

1. If it is truly God's voice then it will generally be related to the text you have read in some way and will not be just some random thought that has crossed your mind.

2. If it is truly God's voice it will never contradict any of God's other words in the Bible.

3. If it is truly God's voice it will most likely be consistent with the clear words of God in Scripture instead of the obscure ones.

4. If it is truly God's voice then what you hear will apply directly to you and your situation, and yield results that are for your good and God's glory.

5. If it is truly God's voice then generally the Church—other believers that you know and trust—will affirm that it is God's voice as well.

6. If it is truly God's voice then it will stand the test of time.

7. As you get to know God better by spending more time with him, your ability to distinguish what is actually God's voice from what is *not* God's voice will improve.

TELLING THE NEW OLD STORY:
TOWARD A BIBLICAL THEOLOGY
OF STORY[85]

I love to tell the story, 'twill be my theme in glory,
to tell the old, old story of Jesus and his love.

Introduction

When I was in college, I went to Daytona Beach in Florida over Spring Break with Campus Crusade for Christ (which is now called Cru). The goal was to do beach evangelism, and they trained us how to use their famous tract, the *Four Spiritual Laws*, to accomplish that goal. The strategy was to approach someone on the beach, engage them in conversation, and then try to find some way to insert that tract into the conversation. We'd never done any beach evangelism before, so we naïvely just lapped up the training. I recall one of us saying, "What if they ask us some really hard questions?" The Campus Crusade person replied, "You guys are going to a Christian college; *you* figure it out." So a few of us thought of ways to apply what we had been learning in class in case we had to use it in a debate, such as Anselm's onto-logical argument for the existence of God or all of the proofs of the resurrection that we had read about in Josh McDowell's book *Evidence that Demands a Verdict*, which was a very popular apologetics text at the time.

After an eighteen-hour van ride we reached Daytona and got up bright and early the next day to hit the beach. One of the first things I noticed was that people had a hard time looking at us because the sun was reflecting off of our pasty white skin. In retrospect I'm convinced that our master evangelism strategy was to *glare* them into the Kingdom. I went up to one guy and started talking to him, and he responded politely enough. Then I whipped out a copy of the *Four Spiritual Laws* and laid one of my evangelism pick-up lines on him: "If you were to die today, why should God let you into his heaven?" And I'll never forget his reaction. He physically fell away from me, as if his body was *involuntarily* recoiling against the suddenness of the question. He seemed to be saying, "OK, you came up to me and started asking me questions as if you wanted to get to know me and be my friend. And then you go and violate that friendship with a question like *that*?" His reaction was typical of what a lot of us ran into on that trip. Here I was, all spun up and ready to go, and I couldn't even win an audience, much less an argument.

Let me flash forward to a more recent conversation. A colleague of mine at work knows that I'm ordained, so he asked me, "What made you want to become a pastor?" I replied, "Let me tell you about a really hard time in grad school when I was finishing off my dissertation and fighting health problems. God used both of those stressful things to give me a call to preach, and to call me to marry the woman who is now my wife." I went on to tell him not only the story of my ordination but also the story of my sanctification, how God had worked in my life over the years to bring me to that point. One of the differences between Daytona Beach and now is that I have replaced syllogism and subterfuge with *story.* And I have discovered that story not only wins me an audience, but it also sustains that audience in a unique way.

Here's a question for you. Let's say your new neighbors invite you over for dinner so that they can get to know the people in the neighborhood. In the course of conversation, they find out not only that you go to church but also that you are a true believer in Jesus Christ. "Why?" they ask you. What do you tell them? Or let's say that a big deadline is coming up at work, and your supervisor asks you to work the weekend to meet it. You respond that you're happy to put in extra time to help out, but that you'd prefer not to work on Sunday mornings so that you can attend church. "Why is church so *important* to you?" he asks. What do you say?

A Reason for the Hope That Is in Us

A well-known passage in 1 Peter chapter 3, verses 13 through 17, encourages us to be ready *in advance* to respond to questions like these. The context of the passage is the reality of suffering for our faith, and the assumption seems to be that the questioners are somewhat antagonistic, which is often the case today.

> Now who is there to harm you if you are zealous for what is good? But even if you should suffer for righteousness' sake, you will be blessed. Have no fear of them, nor be troubled, but in your hearts honor Christ the Lord as holy, always being prepared to make a defense to anyone who asks you for a reason for the hope that is in you; yet do it with gentleness and respect, having a good conscience, so that, when you are slandered, those who revile your good behavior in Christ may be put to shame. For it is better to suffer for doing good, if that should be God's will, than for doing evil.[86]

Let me briefly summarize this passage. Peter passes on four points of advice to those who are suffering for the sake of the gospel. First, don't fear your persecutors or be troubled by them. Second, honor Christ as holy in all that you do. Third, always be prepared to make a defense to anyone who asks you for a reason for the hope that is within you. In other words, *anticipate* this kind of question, and be prepared to respond in advance. Of course, this assumes that people can actually *see* the hope that is within you, that you are truly letting your light shine. Finally, Peter gives a warning that no matter what you say, you should expect to be slandered at times, but that you should live lives that are so unimpeachable, so Christ-like, that those who slander you will be put to shame.

But here's my main point. We often assume that the defense that Peter recommends we prepare in advance—the "reason for the hope that is within us"[87]—is a sustained rational argument, an exercise in apologetics. In the original, the word for "defense" is *apologia*, which was frequently used in a legal context. However, I contend that the reason for the hope that is within us can also be a *story*, not just a logical argument or an intellectual defense; more specifically, it can be *your* story of salvation and growth in grace, or *the* Story of Sin and Redemption. Especially in our postmodern age, which is allergic to proselytizing and any claims to absolute truth, story is a communication medium that will actually *gain* us an audience, unlike (for most people, at least) logical debate or even preaching. And the great thing about story is that it engages the emotions, not just the mind. I've heard it said that if you want someone to *know* the truth, *tell* them the truth. But if you want them to *love* the truth, tell them a *story* about the truth. Story is also subversive, because we can smuggle in absolute truth through the Trojan Horse of our relative experience, and embed the "Old, Old Story" of salvation in our own stories, which ends up telling the *New* Old Story.

Biblical Examples of Story

I'd like to suggest that there are at least three kinds of situations in the Bible itself where the response to questions was a story. The first situation resulted in a *testimony*, a story of someone's life experience. An example of this occurred in the Gospel of John, chapter 9, when on a Sabbath day Jesus healed a man who was born blind.[88] The Pharisees were infuriated, and interrogated the man, then his parents, and then the man again. The ground truth that the Pharisees could not overthrow with their questions was the man's simple story of his own experience: "One thing I do know, that though I was blind, now I see."[89] What I find interesting is that the man didn't allow the Pharisees to trap him into making abstract speculations about Jesus. All of his conclusions about Jesus were based on the concrete facts of the story of his encounter with Jesus. And the Pharisees couldn't argue with the blind man's story, or even with the conclusions that he drew from his story. Why? It was *his* story, *his* experience of Jesus. Besides, he used to be blind, but now he sees. How do you argue with that?

So a personal testimony is one kind of story we see in the Bible in response to questions. A second situation where a story is told in the Bible in response to questions involves the story of *redemption*, the history of salvation itself. An example of this occurred in the Book of Acts, chapter 17, when the apostle Paul was in Athens speaking on Mars Hill to an audience of Epicureans and Stoics.[90] They wanted to hear about his "new teaching,"[91] and he responded by rehearsing the story of redemption for them. But he did so subversively, drawing them in by seeming to appeal to their preconceived ideas of truth, and then unexpectedly providing a gospel twist at the end.

Paul begins his response by praising the religious nature of his audience and identifying their "unknown god"[92] with the creator God of the universe, who made from one man every nation of mankind. The Stoics were probably flattered, and would have been saying to themselves, "Preach it, brother!" because the universal brotherhood of mankind was one of their common themes. Paul continues to support this thesis with quotations from their own poets, and insists that God is near us, not far away, and not locked up in man-made idols of gold or silver fashioned during times of ignorance. By now the Stoics were probably saying to themselves, "Amen! *Somebody*!" because he was hitting their hot buttons—the immanence of God and the ignorance of man. Then came the twist: Paul asserts that this creator God has now called all people to repent, "because he has fixed a day on which he will judge the world in righteousness by a man whom he has appointed; and of this he has given assurance to all by raising him from the dead."[93] The Stoics would have been reeling from this turnabout and scratching their heads in confusion; their view of history was cyclic, not cataclysmic, and they certainly did not believe in a resurrection from the dead in preparation for a final judgment. As a result, some mocked Paul, but others wanted to hear more. The takeaway here is that Paul told a story, the Old, Old Story of redemption and glory. And he told it subversively, drawing them in from a position of common ground and only tugging on the line when the hook was in their mouth. He also told a *better* story than the Stoics did, a *better* narrative of reality that integrated the data of human existence into a more coherent drama of redemption centered on the person and work of Jesus Christ.

Parables

Let me summarize a bit. The answer to questions about "the reason for the hope that is within us"[94] can be a *story*, not just a rational argument. And we see at least three kinds of such stories in the Bible itself. One kind of story we find in the Bible in response to such questions is a story of personal *testimony*. A second kind of story is the story of *redemption*, the history and future of salvation itself through the gospel of Jesus Christ. Now we're ready for a third kind of story, an *indirect* or oblique story, which serves as an indirect response to a sensitive or controversial situation. One example is in Luke chapter 15, where Jesus was accused by the Pharisees and scribes not only of hanging out with sinners, but also of becoming intimate with them by eating with them. Jesus responds indirectly to their allegations by telling them a special kind of story, called a parable, in this case the three familiar parables about Lost and Found. In the first one, Jesus tells the story of a shepherd with a hundred sheep who lost one, and left the ninety-nine in the meadow to scour the land for the one that was lost.[95] When he found it, he not only rejoiced himself but he also invited his friends and neighbors to share his joy. Jesus makes this interesting parenthetical comment at the end of the parable: "Just so, I tell you, there will be more joy in heaven over one sinner who repents than over ninety-nine persons who need no repentance."[96] In the second parable a woman had ten silver coins—the equivalent of a biweekly paycheck—and after she lost one she turned her house upside down until she found it. She too called in her friends and neighbors to rejoice with her.[97] And Jesus made the same kind of parenthetical statement at the end of that parable as well: "Just so, I tell you, there is joy before the angels of God over one sinner who repents."[98] And then comes the most famous Lost and Found parable of all, the Parable of the Prodigal Son.[99] But this one is "Lost and Found with a Twist": the son lost *himself,* and while he was still a long way off, he was found by his *father*, at least in terms of forgiveness, reconciliation, and restoration.

Through these parables, these special kinds of stories, Jesus was *indirectly* telling his accusers that sinners weren't worthless in the sight of God; instead, they were *priceless*, and worthy of dropping everything in order to find and redeem them. Rather than grumbling about Jesus, the Pharisees should be rejoicing, like the angels, that the lost were being found. Because Jesus spoke in parables he didn't come right out and say it, but the implication would have been hard to miss: "You Pharisees and scribes might think that *other* people are sinners, but *you* are sinners too, just like they are. Like them, you have lost *yourselves*, and you need to repent and be found by your Father in heaven."

Emily Dickinson wrote a wonderful poem about just this kind of communication strategy:

> Tell all the Truth but tell it slant —
> Success in Circuit lies
> Too bright for our infirm Delight
> The Truth's superb surprise
> As Lightning to the Children eased
> With explanation kind
> The Truth must dazzle gradually
> Or every man be blind —[100]

Stories and parables are great ways of telling the truth slant, especially if the subject is sensitive or controversial. That's precisely what Jesus did here.

Telling Your Story

At this point you might be asking yourself, "OK, what do I actually *do* with this?" I'd like to make three suggestions, along the lines of the three categories of story that I mentioned earlier. First, always be ready to tell the gospel through your *own* story, *your* story of conversion and growth in grace. You can do this individually—one-on-one with friends or neighbors or colleagues—and you can do this corporately; perhaps you can bake a time of testimony into each Sunday worship service. Let me gently challenge you: What's *your* story of faith? How has *your* life been changed by the gospel, by knowing Jesus Christ as your Savior? Do you know anyone whose story might be changed because you told them *your* story? Second, always be ready to tell the story of redemption and salvation itself, the "Old, Old Story of Jesus and His Love," the "elevator speech" of the gospel. You know what an elevator speech is, right? It's a concise speech that comes to the point quickly and achieves its purpose in the time it takes an elevator to travel from the bottom floor to the top floor, because sometimes that's all the time and opportunity you have with someone. But this begs a question—how well do you know your Bible, especially at an overview level? Can you succinctly summarize the story of redemption, from Genesis to Revelation, as a way of presenting the gospel to someone? My final suggestion is to be prepared to address controversial issues indirectly, through story or parable. Tell the truth of the gospel but tell it *slant*, so that what you have to say will actually be heard. Tell it slant to a world that often only listens slant. Art is a particularly good vehicle for this, so let me encourage you artists out there—fiction writers, songwriters, poets, painters—to continue to communicate gospel truth by telling stories through your art.

Remember—our God is a God of story, because he not only entered the story of humanity in the incarnation and death of his son, but he is writing the story of our own lives even as we speak. What's more, he is writing the story of time itself, and when it reaches the ending that he desires, he will close the book and a new story will begin, the story of eternity in Glory. So let us join together in that great circle of story, where the story of the love within the Godhead spawned the stories of creation, fall, and redemption; where the story of redemption in Jesus intersects with our own story; and where our own story intersects with the story of others; to come continually full circle by magnifying the glory of God and reinforcing the bonds of love within the Trinity.

ENDNOTES

[1] Psalm 5:3
[2] Mark 1:35
[3] Psalm 1:1-3
[4] James 1:22-25
[5] Psalm 119:97, 103-104
[6] John 1:1
[7] John 1:1-8
[8] 1 Samuel 3:10
[9] Philippians 4:4-9
[10] Philippians 4:4
[11] Romans 8:28
[12] Philippians 4:5a
[13] Philippians 4:5b
[14] Philippians 4:9
[15] Matthew 6:9-13
[16] 2 Samuel 11:1-12:24
[17] Psalm 51:10
[18] Philippians 1:3-11
[19] Philippians 1:3
[20] Psalm 150
[21] Psalm 23
[22] Psalm 19:14
[23] Psalm 51:10
[24] Psalm 119:57-60
[25] Psalm 119:11
[26] John 14:26
[27] Matthew 4:1-11
[28] Deuteronomy 8:3; Deuteronomy 6:16; Deuteronomy 6:13.

[29] Ephesians 6:11-18a
[30] Joshua 4:19-24
[31] Psalm 91:1-8
[32] Psalm 91:9-16
[33] Ephesians 1:13-14; 1 Corinthians 6:19-20.
[34] Romans 8:26-27
[35] Hebrews 8:1-2; Hebrews 12:1-2.
[36] Romans 8:34
[37] Hebrews 4:14-16
[38] Ephesians 1:15-23
[39] Luke 18:9-14
[40] Luke 18:38
[41] Luke 18:14a; Luke 18:42-43.
[42] 1 Thessalonians 5:16-18
[43] 1 Thessalonians 5:17
[44] In some circles it is pronounced "**lex**-ee-oh di-**vee**-na."
[45] Psalm 1:2
[46] Psalm 46:10
[47] 1 Samuel 3:10
[48] Psalm 19:14; Psalm 51:10.
[49] Psalm 119:18
[50] 2 Corinthians 2:6-16
[51] Philippians 4:4-9
[52] Philippians 3:1
[53] Philippians 4:7
[54] Philippians 4:11-12
[55] Philippians 4:13
[56] Philippians 4:4
[57] Philippians 1:27-28
[58] Philippians 3:2-3
[59] Philippians 4:2-3
[60] Philippians 2:3-11
[61] 1 Samuel 3:10
[62] Philippians 1:6
[63] 1 Samuel 3:10
[64] Psalm 19
[65] Psalm 19:1-6
[66] Psalm 19:7-11
[67] Psalm 19:12-14

68 Matthew 6:13

69 Psalm 19:14a

70 Psalm 19:14

71 2 Peter 1:21

72 Psalm 98:8

73 Matthew 24:36

74 Mark 3:28-29

75 Ephesians 1:13-14; 1 Peter 1:5.

76 Isaiah 35:3. See also Hebrews 12:12.

77 Exodus 23:20

78 John 10:27

79 1 Timothy 1:2, New International Version (NIV).

80 2 Timothy 3:14–17

81 Hebrews 4:12–13

82 Psalm 119:97

83 Matthew 6:9-13

84 1 Thessalonians 5:17

85 An earlier version of this appendix was posted online at http://north-amanglican.com/telling-the-new-old-story-towards-a-biblical-theology-of-story.

86 1 Peter 3:13-17

87 1 Peter 3:15

88 John 9:1-41

89 John 9:25b

90 Acts 17:16-34

91 Acts 17:19

92 Acts 17:23

93 Acts 17:31

94 1 Peter 3:15

95 Luke 15:4-6

96 Luke 15:7

97 Luke 15:8-9

98 Luke 15:10

99 Luke 15:11-32

100 Ralph W. Franklin, ed., *The Poems of Emily Dickinson: Reading Edition* (Cambridge, MA, and London, England: The Belknap Press of Harvard University Press, 1998, 1999), poem 1263, p. 494.

Made in the USA
Lexington, KY
11 December 2019